Airline
of the
1980s

Gerry Manning

MIDLAND
An imprint of
Ian Allan Publishing

First published 2007

ISBN (10) 1 85780 261 6
ISBN (13) 978 1 85780 261 0

© Gerry Manning 2007

Published by Midland Publishing

Midland Publishing is an imprint of
Ian Allan Publishing Ltd
Riverdene Business Park, Molesey Road,
Hersham, Surrey, KT12 4RG

Worldwide distribution (except North America):
Midland Counties Publications
4 Watling Drive, Hinckley, LE10 3EY, England
Telephone: 01455 254 450   Fax: 01455 233 737
E-mail: midlandbooks@compuserve.com
www.midlandcountiessuperstore.com

North American trade distribution:
Specialty Press Publishers & Wholesalers Inc.
39966 Grand Avenue, North Branch, MN 55056
Tel: 651 277 1400   Fax: 651 277 1203
Toll free telephone: 800 895 4585
www.specialtypress.com

Layout by Russell Strong

Printed in England
by Ian Allan Printing Ltd
Riverdene Business Park, Molesey Road,
Hersham, Surrey, KT12 4RG

Visit the Ian Allan Publishing website at:
www.ianallanpublishing.com

Introduction

This book is a follow-up to my 2005 *Airliners of the 1970s*. The basic premise
is the same, to illustrate the range of both airliners and airlines that operated
during the decade. It is of course impossible within the scope of a book this
size to cover all the types and carriers that flew during those years.

What I have tried to do is to cover as wide a selection of aircraft types and
their operators over as large a geographical spread as possible, from the small
commuters to the large wide-bodies.

The decade saw many new airlines that came and went within a few short
years. This short lifespan of some airlines happens in all countries of the world:
many times in the text the words 'operations were suspended' appear. This
was also a decade that saw Europe resume a leading role in the supply of
airliners with the growth of the Airbus consortium.

With the captions I have attempted to note who the airline was, or still is,
what the aeroplane type was, and where and when the picture was taken.
Finally I outline the fate of the illustrated aircraft.

Acknowledgements

I am indebted to Bob O'Brien for filling in some of the gaps in my travels with
slides from assorted parts of the world. Pictures without a credit are my own.
Thanks also to Bill Hodgson of Aerodata for filling in many of the fates of the
various aircraft.

Gerry Manning
Liverpool

Title page photograph:

British Caledonian first operated the DC-10 in
March 1977 on its routes to Africa. A total of ten
were operated by the airline. Pictured landing at
Los Angeles-LAX in September 1988 is DC-10-30
G-BHDJ (c/n 47840). In April of that year the
company had been taken over by British Airways.
This aircraft was sold on, converted to a freighter,
and is currently in service with a Miami-based
company.

The first aircraft from the Airbus consortium of companies to enter service was the A300. It was a twin-engine, wide-body airliner with a seating capacity, dependent on layout, of between 250 and 360 seats. To crack the very protected US market Airbus leased four aircraft for six months, free of charge, to Eastern Air Lines. This proved the popularity of the type and the carrier's fleet grew to thirty-five aircraft. Pictured at Miami in October 1981 is Airbus A300B4-103 N219EA (c/n 120) of Eastern Air Lines. This company was one of the high-profile failures among major US carriers when operations were finally suspended in January 1991. This airframe was sold on to Alitalia, withdrawn from use and stored in Rome, and later broken up for spare parts.

Once the largest independent airline in Europe, Dan-Air was set up in 1953, with the name being derived from its shipping broker owners Davis and Newman. It was eventually taken over by British Airways in 1992. Pictured at London-Gatwick in July 1987 is Airbus A300B4-103 G-BMNB (c/n 009). This airframe was withdrawn from use at Toulouse, France, the site of the Airbus factory, in 1997 and eventually broken up for spares recovery.

Air Jamaica was the first operator of the A300 in the Caribbean region. They flew services to points in the USA and Canada. At Miami in June 1989 is Airbus A300B4-203 F-BVGP (c/n 145). This aircraft was withdrawn from use and stored at Paris-Orly Airport in 1994, and used for fire practice in 2000.

Using a leased Air France machine Air Seychelles flew services from Mahé to several European locations. Pictured at London-Gatwick in July 1987 is Airbus A300B4-203 F-BVGM (c/n 078). In 1999 the airframe was converted to a freighter by BAe and is currently operated by a Mexican carrier.

Owned by Horizon Travel, Orion Airways flew holiday charters for its parent company. They operated the A300 for just over a year before being taken over by Thomson Holidays and merged into Britannia Airways during 1989 when the Airbuses were sold. Landing at London-Gatwick in July 1988 is A300B4-203 G-BMZL (c/n 077). It was sold on to Iberia, being later withdrawn and broken for spare parts at La Munoza during 1999.

The Italian flag carrier Alitalia first operated Airbus aircraft in 1981 and has continued to do so ever since. Seen at its Rome base in June 1988 is Airbus A300B4-203 I-BUSF (c/n 123). Sold on, it was converted to a freighter in 1997 and is currently operated by a Turkish carrier.

Like most manufacturers Airbus constantly improves its designs. The -600 version had a stretch of 21in (53.34cm), a new 'glass cockpit' that did away with the need for a flight engineer, and many other modifications. Pictured at Miami in July 1989 is Airbus A300-605R N70054 (c/n 461) of American Airlines. The 'R' in its designation indicated a long-range version with a 1,620 US gallon (6,130 litres) fuel tank in the horizontal stabiliser. This gave the aircraft a 180-minute ETOPS (Extended Range Twin Operations) capability. This airframe still serves with the carrier.

The Airbus A310 was an A300 with the fuselage shortened by 22ft 8in (6.9m) and a smaller wing area. It had a seating capacity of 280 and first flew in April 1982. It had a longer range than the A300, with the -300 variant being able to fly over 5,000 miles. **Balair** was a Swiss holiday charter airline owned by Swissair. As their parent company was one of the launch customers, together with Lufthansa, it was natural for one to be operated by Balair. At its Zurich base, in August 1987, is Airbus A310-322 HB-IPK (c/n 412). Balair were merged with CTA to form Balair/CTA and later absorbed into the parent. This aircraft was sold on and operated in Kazakhstan, it was eventually reduced to spares in France during 2006.

Dubai-based **Emirates Airlines** only started operations in 1985 and in the intervening years has grown to be the dominant carrier in the area, expanding its influence across the world. The carrier operated a fleet of ten A310s, with the first being delivered in July 1987. Seen at London-Gatwick in that month is Airbus A310-304 A6-EKA (c/n 432). Sold on ten years later, it was operated in France and reduced to spares in the USA during 2004.

In the world of airline cabin service **Singapore Airlines** is in a class of its own. The flag carrier for the small island nation operated a total of twenty-three A310s on its routes around its Asian neighbours. Pictured at Bangkok in November 1989 is Airbus A310-324 9V-STP (c/n 443). It was sold in 2000, stored at Mojave in August 2003 and later broken up there.

Thai Airways have operated large numbers of Airbus A300s but only small numbers of the shorter A310, these having an all-economy seating capacity of 265 for use on high-capacity domestic routes. At Phuket in November 1989 is Airbus A310-204 HS-TIC (c/n 424). Sold on, this airframe was broken up for spares during 2001.

Turkish flag carrier THY-Turk Hava Yollari (Turkish Airlines) received its first A310 in May 1985 and still operates the type in reduced numbers today. Pictured at Zurich in August 1987, in the carrier's old colours, is Airbus A310-203 TC-JCO (c/n 386). This is one of the aircraft that is still in service with THY.

First flown in February 1987 the Airbus A320 was the first of a whole family of narrow-body, single-aisle airliners from the consortium. They have taken on the world's best-selling airliner, the Boeing 737, and carved a huge share of that market. April 1988 saw the first passenger services with Air France. In service at London-Gatwick in July 1988 is Airbus A320-110 G-BUSC (c/n 008) of British Airways. This carrier had for many years been almost a 'Boeing-only' company but, following their takeover of British Caledonian in 1988, they inherited a small order for A320s. Having operated these the carrier now has in service or on order seventy-nine of the single-aisle family. This aircraft is still in service with BA but scheduled to be retired at the end of 2007 when it will be reduced to spare parts.

The Grumman G.159 Gulfstream 1 was a twin-engine, Rolls-Royce Dart-powered aircraft sold in the business executive market place. A small number have been operated as airliners seating twenty-four passengers. Pictured at Birmingham-Elmdon in July 1988 is Gulfstream 1 G-BMOW (c/n 155) of Birmingham Executive Airways. The company changed its name to Birmingham European Airways and this aircraft was sold in the Democratic Republic of Congo where it is believed to still operate.

One of the most remarkable airlines flying today was set up in the 1980s. This is JU-Air. They obtained three genuine Junkers-built tri-motors from the Swiss Air Force, which had operated them since 1939, and employ them on sightseeing and pleasure flights through the Swiss Alps. Pictured landing at Zurich, in August 1987 is Junkers Ju52/3m HB-HOP (c/n 6610). Both aircraft and carrier still fly to this day.

Based at Toronto Island Airport, **City Express** was a Canadian commuter airline. Pictured in July 1986 at Hamilton, Ontario is Saunders ST.27 C-FFZP (c/n 010/14070). This aircraft was a conversion of the de Havilland DH.114 Heron. Two 715shp PT-6A turboprops replaced the four Gipsy Queen piston engines, the fuselage was increased in length, the wing re-engineered and the nose extended, amongst other modifications. The Canadian company of Saunders converted twenty airframes. City Express ceased operations in 1991 and this aircraft was stored at the airline's base in 1988 and broken up the same year.

The last flying design from the British manufacturer Handley Page was the HP.137 Jetstream, an 18/20-seat commuter airliner. First flown in August 1967 it was powered by a pair of 850shp Turbomeca Astazou turboprops. Good advanced sales were made in the American market before the company had to call in the receiver and cease production. Pictured at Albuquerque, New Mexico in October 1984 is HP.137 Jetstream Mk.1 N114CP (c/n 202) of locally based **JetAire Airlines**. This carrier ceased operations in January 1986 and the aircraft is now at the Netherlands Luchtvaart College at Hoofddorp being used as an instructional airframe. (The four aircraft in formation in the background are F-16s of the USAF 'Thunderbirds' team.)

Since the Jetstream was a sound design it was put into production by British Aerospace's Scottish Division at Prestwick. Nearly 400 aircraft were built. The new product had a pair of 1020shp TPE 331 turboprops fitted. Pictured at Manchester-Ringway in September 1984 is BAe 3011 Jetstream 31 G-BKHI (c/n 604) of Scottish commuter and air taxi operator **Peregrine Air Services**. In 1989 the company changed its name to Aberdeen Airways. This airframe operated in Scandinavia before sale to a US owner.

Built in Australia and powered by three 145hp Gipsy Major piston engines the de Havilland Drover was a six- to eight-seat feeder airliner whose most famous operator was the Royal Flying Doctor Service. It was first flown in January 1948 and twenty aircraft were built. Pictured in May 1985 at Auckland, New Zealand is DHA.3 Drover ZK-DDD (c/n 5019) of locally based **Great Barrier Airlines**. This carrier is still currently operating and its largest aircraft is a Britten-Norman Trislander. This aircraft is currently in the Australian Aviation Museum at Sydney. (It is of note that this New Zealand-registered aircraft only carries the last three letters of its registration 'DDD'. The absence of national prefix 'ZK' indicates that the aircraft did not leave national airspace.) (Bob O'Brien)

A turboprop commuter with up to twenty seats, the Dornier Do 228 was first flown in March 1981 with production in both Germany and under licence by Hindustan in India. Pictured landing at the Farnborough Air Show in September 1984 is Dornier Do 228-200 D-IASX (c/n 8035) of German commuter airline **Delta Air**. This carrier was renamed Deutsche BA in June 1992 while the aircraft is still currently flying for German company LGW as D-ILWB.

The Piper Navajo is a six- to eight-seat low-wing cabin monoplane that has been sold in the thousands and has been developed into many variants. Pictured at Santa Rosa, California in September 1988 is PA-31 Navajo N45014 (c/n 31-8052171) of **Ameriflight**. The carrier has a large fleet of aircraft up to the size of a Brasilia all flying freight around the western states of the USA. The pictured aircraft is still one of them.

Based in Billings, Montana **Big Sky Airlines** is a small commuter carrier. Seen at base in August 1986 is Cessna 402C N5826C (c/n 0050). The Cessna 400 series of twin-engine aircraft serves both the private and commuter markets, seating up to nine passengers. This aircraft still flies in the USA, albeit no longer in airline use.

Swedish aerospace company SAAB (Svenska Aeroplan Aktiebolaget AB) are best known for their very high-tech fighters, which have equipped the national air force since World War II. Their first airliner was the 1950s Scandia, of which only eighteen airframes were constructed. Far more success was achieved with the SF340 regional airliner. Turboprop-powered, this thirty-five seater aircraft first flew in January 1983 and entered service the following year with Swiss carrier Crossair. At the carrier's Zurich base in August 1987 is Saab SF340A HB-AHC (c/n 340A-009). In 2002, following the shock collapse of Swissair, Crossair was renamed Swiss International Air Lines after taking over what was left of the national carrier. This aircraft was sold on to Egyptian carrier Raslan Air, via the USA in July 2000. Registered SU-PAB, it has since been withdrawn from use in Egypt.

A franchise operator, Express Airlines flew commuters for Minneapolis/ St Paul-based Republic Airlines under the name of Republic Express. Pictured at base in July 1986 is Saab SF340A N324PX (c/n 340A-048). During that year Republic Airlines was taken over by Northwest Airlines, also based at MSP. The company became a Northwest Airlink carrier and the aircraft served with them until being placed in storage at Bangor, Maine.

Isle of Man-based Manx Airlines was established in 1982 flying scheduled passenger services. They were part of the British Regional Airlines Group and in 2002 were merged into British Airways Citiexpress. Pictured landing at Liverpool-Speke in April 1987 is Saab SF340A G-HOPP (c/n 340A-008). This aircraft can currently be found operating regional services in New South Wales, Australia.

Eastern Express was the commuter feeder for Miami-based Eastern Air Lines operated by a number of regional airlines with aircraft in livery. Pictured at Boston, Massachusetts in August 1986 is Saab SF340A N404BH (c/n 340A-061). When, in January 1991, the main carrier ceased operations so did the Express divisions. This aircraft was withdrawn and stored in the USA for a period of time, converted to a freighter and is currently operated by a Miami-based carrier.

Launched at the 1981 Paris Air Show French and Italian manufacturers Aerospatiale and Aeritalia formed ATR (Avion de Transport Regional) to build a mid-size commuter aircraft. First flown in August 1984, the component manufacture was split between the two nations and final assembly was in France at Toulouse. Pictured departing Washington-National in May 1989 is ATR 42-300 N144DD (c/n 074) of American Eagle, the regional feeder for American Airlines. The '42' was so named because of the seating capacity. The airframe was withdrawn and stored, then broken up for spare parts in 2002.

With a history dating back to 1919 Chalk's International Airlines could claim to be one of the world's oldest carriers. Miami-based, they flew to the Bahamas operating flying boats off some of the world's most scenic waterways. Pictured at Paradise Island, Nassau in the Bahamas, in October 1981, is Grumman G.73 Mallard N2970 (c/n J.28). The Mallard was the third in a line of amphibians built by the company and had a production run of fifty-nine aircraft. The carrier is now called Chalk's Ocean Airways and this aircraft was sold to a private individual.

The Mallard was often regarded as underpowered so a number had their 600hp Pratt & Whitney Wasp radial pistons replaced with 652shp PT-6A turboprops. Pictured in October 1981 at Bimini in the Bahamas is G-73 Turbo Mallard N2969 (c/n J.27) of Chalk's International Airlines as it taxies down the ramp into the water. Sadly this aircraft was destroyed in a fatal crash in December 2005.

The Shorts 330 was a thirty-seat commuter airliner that grew out of the SC.7 Skyvan. First flown in August 1974, power was supplied by a pair of PT-6A-45 1120shp turboprops. Pictured at Liverpool-Speke in April 1984 is Short 330 G-BKSV (c/n SH.3096) in the livery of **Air Ecosse**. This Aberdeen-based Scottish carrier suspended operations in January 1987 and was taken over by Peregrine Air Services the following year. In April 1990 this aircraft was destroyed by a terrorist bomb whilst stored at Belfast.

Humberside-based **Genair** operated commuter services for British Caledonian and carried the markings of both companies. Pictured at Liverpool-Speke in April 1983 is Shorts 330 G-EASI (c/n SH.3070). BCal was taken over by British Airways in 1988. Genair had suspended operations in July 1984. This aircraft was withdrawn from use in 1998 and broken up the following year.

Seen at Washington-National in May 1989 is Short 330-200 N412CA (c/n SH.3016) of **Allegheny Commuter**. This carrier operated feeder services for US Air and now operates in the livery of US Airways Express. This aircraft was damaged beyond economic repair by high winds on the Pacific island of Guam in August 1992.

Developed from the 330 the Shorts 360 first flew in June 1981. It had a stretched fuselage, single fin and uprated engines. Pictured in store at Pinal Air Park, Marana, Arizona in October 1984 is Shorts 360-100 N131DA (c/n SH.3631) of **Dash Air**. The Santa Ana, California-based carrier had suspended services earlier that year. This aircraft was later operated by an airline in Panama.

Manx Airlines had a contract to fly overnight post for the Royal Mail. To advertise both Data Post and Royal Mail Special Services Shorts 360-100 G-RMSS (c/n SH.3604) received a special livery and registration. It is pictured at Liverpool-Speke in April 1986. This aircraft was later operated in the UK by Emerald Airways until their suspension of operations in May 2006 and then stored.

Once run as a separate division of the parent company **Aer Lingus Commuter** was incorporated into the main body in October 1998. Pictured at Liverpool-Speke in April 1986 is Shorts 360-100 EI-BEK (c/n SH.3635). This aircraft now operates freight flights for UK carrier BAC Express.

Pictured at Marana, Arizona in October 1984 is Shorts 360-100 N913SB (c/n SH.3629) of Arkansas-based commuter and air taxi carrier **Sunbelt Airlines**. The aircraft was in temporary store as the company has suspended operations that month. This airframe was later converted to a C-23B Sherpa for the US Army.

US domestic carrier Piedmont Airlines has grown following the deregulation of America's airlines, they now fly as US Airways. Pictured operating local regional services is **Piedmont Commuter** Shorts 360-300 N722PC (c/n SH.3722). It is at the carrier's Charlotte, South Carolina base in May 1989. Converted to a freighter, this aircraft currently operates in Puerto Rico.

A joint development between Fairchild and Swearingen, the Metro was a 19-seater powered by a pair of Garrett TPE.331 turboprops. It first flew in 1969. Seen at Oshkosh, Wisconsin in August 1986 is SA-227AC Metro III N192MA (c/n AC-476) of Midstate Airlines. This carrier suspended services in January 1989 and the pictured aircraft is currently a freighter for a west coast American carrier.

Terre Haute, Indiana-based Britt Airways took its name from founder Bill Britt. Pictured in July 1986 at Dayton, Ohio is SA-226TC Metro II N325BA (c/n TC-304). The carrier became part of Continental Express and the aircraft was sold to a company based in Missouri.

The commuter arm of TWA, Trans World Express was, as so many are, a franchise operation. One such franchise was operated by Wilkes-Barre, Pennsylvania-based Pocono Airlines. Pictured at Washington-National in May 1989 is SA-227AC Metro III N3107P (c/n AC-496). Pocono suspended operations in January 1990 and this aircraft was sold in South America, being destroyed in a landing accident in Peru in November 2000.

American commuter carrier SkyWest Airlines currently operates a franchise for two of the giants of America's airlines, United and Delta. Pictured at Santa Barbara, California in September 1988 in their own livery is SA-227AC Metro III N3114G (c/n AC-583). This airframe currently operates as a freighter in Montana.

SA-227AC Metro III N343AE (c/n AC-554) of American Eagle is pictured at Lake Tahoe, Nevada in September 1988. Sold on, this aircraft was damaged beyond economic repair at Hawthorne , California in September 2002.

Antigua-based **4 Island Air Services** was a scheduled passenger carrier in the Caribbean. Pictured at base in June 1983 is Britten-Norman BN-2A Islander V2-LAG (c/n 163). First flown in June 1965 the design was a ten-seater able to operate from unprepared strips and simple to operate in the field with regard to maintenance. 4 Island was a subsidiary of LIAT (Leeward Islands Air Transport) and was absorbed into the main carrier in 1986. The pictured aircraft is operated by a company in St Vincent & Grenadines. (Bob O'Brien)

Air Seychelles is the flag carrier for the island nation. Founded in 1979 long-haul operations are currently flown by a pair of Boeing 767s. Pictured in June 1983 at its Mahé base is Britten-Norman BN-2A Mk.111 Trislander S7-AAN (c/n 1026). The Trislander was an eighteen-seater with a stretched fuselage and a third engine mounted in the fin. This aircraft was sold to a UK operator, being eventually withdrawn and stored in Guernsey in 1998 before use by the fire service at Alderney. (Bob O'Brien)

Bristol-based **Aviation West** flew both newspapers and post during night operations around the UK. Pictured at Liverpool-Speke in June 1985 is BN-2A-III Trislander G-AZLJ (c/n 0319). The carrier ceased operations the following year while this airframe was withdrawn from use at Coventry in 2001 and the fuselage used for spares at Lydd, and ended its days in a scrap yard at Chatham.

The Beech 99 was a seventeen-seat commuter airliner that was developed from the Queen Air range of executive transports. First flown in October 1966 it was turboprop powered. Pictured at Los Angeles-LAX in September 1984 is Beech 99A N51PA (c/n U-80) of Long Beach-based Desert Sun Airlines. The carrier ceased operations in 1987. This aircraft was converted to a freighter and is currently operated in Minnesota.

Beech grew its range with the model 1900. This was a 21-seat commuter airliner powered by a pair of 850shp P&W Canada PT-6A turboprops. It first flew in September 1982. Pictured at Albany, New York, in July 1986 is Beech 1900C N809BE (c/n UB-40) of Bridgeport, Connecticut-based Business Express. This carrier became part of Delta Connection while the aircraft eventually went to Sudan where it is now for sale.

The de Havilland Canada DHC-3 Otter is one of the great 'bush' aircraft of the world. They fly off wheels, skis and floats depending upon the season and location, while many have been fitted with turboprop power plants. Pictured in September 1984 at Vancouver Airport Sea Plane Base is Powell River-based Powell Air DHC-3 Otter C-FXUY (c/n 142). The carrier merged with Pacific Coastal Airlines in 1988. This aircraft has since been fitted with a turboprop engine and currently operates on wheels for a Yellowknife-based carrier.

First flown in 1937, the Beech 18 had a production run of thirty-two years, the line not closing until 1969. Pictured at Renton, Washington in August 1986 is Beech 18C N1047B (c/n 7728). It is operated by Alaskan Coastal Airways based at Juneau. The carrier suspended services in 1997 and this aircraft is now preserved at the Alaska Aviation Heritage Museum in Anchorage.

The bulk of the production of the de Havilland Canada Caribou was sold to the world's air forces. Those that have adopted civil markings are to be found in freight operations. Pictured in September 1988 at Sacramento Executive Airport, California is DHC-4A Caribou N544Y (c/n 241) of based Union Flights. This small parcel carrier suspended operations in 2005, this airframe having passed into dereliction in South Africa by 2000.

Spanish manufacturer CASA (Construcciones Aeronauticas SA) was founded in 1923. Early production was licensed copies of mainly German designs. Together with Indonesian company Nurtanio they have produced the CN.235 turboprop airliner. It first flew in November 1983 and has a seating capacity for forty-four passengers. Pictured at the Farnborough Air Show in September 1988, prior to delivery, is CASA CN.235 EC-011 (c/n 006) of Canary Island-based Binter Canarias. This carrier currently flies around the various islands of the group. After delivery the aircraft took the registration EC-EMO but has since been withdrawn, stored and cancelled from the Spanish register upon delivery to the Turkish Army.

De Havilland Canada first flew the DHC-6 Twin Otter in May 1965; it was a nineteen-seat, turboprop-powered, high-wing, fixed undercarriage commuter that eventually sold over 800 machines. Pictured on the ramp at Antigua in June 1983 is DHC-6 Twin Otter 300 VP-LMD (c/n 728) of **Montserrat Air Services**. This carrier was based at Plymouth, the capital of the island of Montserrat, one of the Leeward Islands of the Caribbean. The airline ceased operations in 1988 and this aircraft was later flying in Angola. (Bob O'Brien)

Vancouver-based **Air BC** flew its aircraft off both land and water in its operations around British Columbia. Pictured under maintenance at base in September 1984 is de Havilland Canada DHC-6 Twin Otter 200 C-FPAE (c/n 228). The carrier became a subsidiary of Air Canada and this aircraft is now used as a platform for US skydivers.

Haiti Air Inter was a small Port au Prince-based commuter carrier. Pictured at Miami in October 1981 is DHC-6 Twin Otter 200 HH-AIY (c/n 188). The airline ceased services in 1984 and sold the aircraft to the Haiti Air Force. Sold on again, it was damaged beyond economic repair in Florida during 1999.

Formed in 1969 Brazilian manufacturer Embraer (Empresa Brasileira de Aeronautica SA) has gone from strength to strength selling its airliners worldwide. Its first success was the EMB-110 Bandeirante. This first flew in 1972 and was a turboprop-powered nineteen-passenger commuter airliner. Pictured at Liverpool-Speke in June 1981 is EMB-110P2 Bandeirante G-BHYT (c/n 110277) of Humberside-based Genair. The carrier suspended operations in July 1984 and this aircraft was sold in Canada and then withdrawn from use and stored.

South African carrier Mmabatho Air Services was based in Mafeking in what was then the Republic of Bophuthatswana, a semi-independent tribal homeland. Pictured in May 1986 at Johannesburg-Jan Smuts is EMB-110P1 Bandeirante ZS-LGP (c/n 110402). The following year the carrier was renamed Bopair and this aircraft was destroyed in a crash while with them in March 1988. (Bob O'Brien)

Pictured at Miami in June 1989 is EMB-110P1 Bandeirante N64CZ (c/n 110399) of American commuter carrier Comair. Now an all-jet airline they fly as Delta Connection, a subsidiary of Delta Air Lines. This aircraft now operates as a freighter for a Vermont-based company.

Embraer followed the Bandeirante with the much sleeker Brasilia. First flown in July 1983, it was a thirty-passenger commuter with a T-tail and a pair of 1800shp P&W PW.118 turboprops. Pictured landing at Santa Barbara, California in September 1988 is EMB-120 Brasilia N270UE (c/n 120026) in the livery of United Express. The owner was Fresno-based Westair Commuter Airlines who were a franchise carrier for United Airlines. This aircraft was withdrawn and stored in 1998 and broken up for spare parts in 2003.

The CASA C.212 has sold well to the air forces of the world that need a rugged, easy to maintain, turboprop-powered, small cargo aircraft. It has also found limited use in the civil market as a feederliner seating up to nineteen passengers. Pictured at Boston in August 1986 is CASA C.212-200 N451AM (c/n 165) of Hyannis, Massachusetts-based Gull Air. In March 1987 the carrier suspended services and this aircraft now flies as a freighter for a company in Wyoming.

Few airliners have been designed to have STOL (Short Take-Off and Landing) capability. One such was the de Havilland Canada DHC-7 Dash 7. First flown in March 1975 it had four turboprop engines and a fifty-seat capacity. Pictured at East Midlands-Castle Donington in July 1989 is DHC-7-110 G-BOAX (c/n 111) of London City Airways. This carrier was part of the Airlines of Great Britain Group and in October 1990 merged into the parent company, British Midland. This aircraft can now be found in the cold of the Antarctic as a survey aircraft.

Pictured landing at New York-JFK in May 1989 is DHC-7 Dash 7-102 N175RA (c/n 56) in the livery of Pan Am Express. This Philadelphia-based airline operated the feeder services for Pan Am. When the parent ceased operations in 1991 so did the Express division. This aircraft joined the US Army and is currently stored in Texas.

Based in Innsbruck, Austrian carrier Tyrolean Airways operated scheduled passenger services around western Europe. Pictured landing at Zurich in August 1987 is DHC-7 Dash 7-102 OE-LLS (c/n 22). The airline now flies as Austrian Arrows as it is now owned by the national flag carrier Austrian Airlines. This aircraft was broken up for spare parts in Guernsey, Channel Islands during 2001 following a period of storage.

Operating passenger services from Florida to the Bahamas, DHC-7 Dash 7-102 N780MG (c/n 80) of Paradise Island Airways is pictured landing at Miami in June 1989. At that time they were part of Chalk's and eventually flew as a US Air Express company. This aircraft can currently be found in passenger service in Kenya.

De Havilland Canada followed the Dash 7 with the Dash 8. This was a twin-turboprop that has grown through three fuselage lengths: seating from forty in the -100 series, to fifty-six in the -300, and seventy-eight in the latest -400 series. Pictured at Phoenix, Arizona in September 1988 is DHC-8 Dash 8-102 N804AW (c/n 082) of based America West Airlines. This carrier was the dominant partner in the 2005 merger with US Air but chose to adopt that name for its new operations. This aircraft was withdrawn and stored in Nevada during 2002 and cancelled from the register, the fuselage is now at London, Ontario.

Salisbury, Maryland-based Henson Airlines was a commuter carrier operating services for Piedmont. Pictured at Washington-National in May 1989 is DHC-8 Dash 8-102 N916HA (c/n 072). The carrier is now part of US Air Express and this aircraft is in store.

Founded in 1985, Bangkok Airways have grown from flying a single Bandeirante on domestic operations to operating single-aisle Airbus aircraft on regional international services. Pictured at its Bangkok-Don Muang base, in November 1989, is DHC-8 Dash 8-103 HS-SKH (c/n 144). This aircraft currently serves with a Caribbean airline.

First flown in May 1963, the Dassault Falcon 20 was the first in a long line of French business jets. Over time older ones have been converted to carry small items of freight. Pictured at Detroit-Willow Run in July 1986 is based Reliant Airlines Falcon 20DC N212R (c/n 212). This carrier specialised in flying motor industry components to plants around the country. Operations were suspended in 2002 and this aircraft does the same job for another locally based company.

When one looks at their vast fleet of several hundred aircraft, many of them wide-body, it is hard to believe that Federal Express (now known as FedEx) once ran with a small fleet of business jet aircraft. Falcon 20D N18FE (c/n 233) is pictured at Marana, Arizona, in October 1984. This aircraft is currently used by a freight company moving motor parts around the USA.

Built as a heavy lift helicopter for the US Army, the Sikorsky S-64 Skycrane first flew in May 1962. It was able to lift a specially designed cargo pod or use its high undercarriage to straddle items to be lifted and was known in the service as the H-54 Tarhe. As they have been slowly phased out of service some have been acquired by specialist companies working in the lumber industry or as water bombers protecting forests. One such is California-based Siller Bros. Pictured at Detroit-Willow Run in July 1986 is S-64E Skycrane N4035S (c/n 64099). This machine still serves with the company.

A development from the UH-1, the Bell 212 was powered by a P&W Canada PT-6A Twin Pac of 1290shp, it first flew in April 1965 and saw service in both civil and military fields. Pictured at Vancouver, British Columbia in September 1984 is Bell 212 C-GLZG (c/n 31130) of based Highland Helicopters. This model is no longer operated by the company and this airframe is now in service with a passenger carrier in India.

Powered by a pair of Soloviev D-30 turbofans with 14,990lb of static thrust, the Tupolev Tu-134 was a short-haul airliner that first flew in July 1963. It was widely used in the USSR, its satellites, and countries under their influence. Pictured at Bangkok in November 1989 is Tu-134A VN-A110 (c/n 62144) of **Hang Khong Vietnam**, the national flag carrier and in fact the only airline in the country at that time. They have since renamed themselves Vietnam Airlines and this aircraft was withdrawn from use during the 1990s.

Interflug was the sole airline of the old German Democratic Republic (East Germany). Following the reunification of the country it suspended operations in 1991 and its fleet of gas-guzzling Russian-built airliners were disposed of. Pictured at Manchester-Ringway in May 1988 is Tupolev Tu-134A DDR-SCX (c/n 48320). This aircraft was sold to a Russian carrier and still serves with them.

Belgrade-based **Aviogenex** have survived all the troubles and turmoil of the break-up of the old state of Yugoslavia and continue to operate albeit now with western-built aircraft. Pictured at Zurich, in August 1987, is Tupolev Tu-134A YU-AJA (c/n 1206). This aircraft was sold to a Russian carrier and cancelled from the register in 1997.

Scaled up from the Tu-134, the Tupolev Tu-154 was powered by three tail-mounted Kuznetsov NK-8 turbofans. Medium-range, it could seat up to 167 passengers in the original variant and first flew in October 1968. Pictured at London-Heathrow, in May 1988, is Tu-154B-2 YR-TPJ (c/n 408) of **Tarom**, the Romanian flag carrier. They, like most former eastern-bloc countries, now have a fleet of western-built aircraft. The pictured machine crashed at Otopeni in February 1989.

Pictured at Zurich, in August 1987, is Tupolev Tu-154B HA-LCG (c/n 127) of Hungarian national airline **Malev**. The Budapest-based carrier now operates an all western-built fleet. This aircraft has been preserved at the transport museum at Ferihegy Airfield.

The Tu-154M was an upgraded version with new Aviadvigatel D-30KU turbofans of 23,150lb static thrust and other equipment changes. Pictured at London-Heathrow in May 1988 is Tupolev Tu-154M SP-LCA (c/n 727) of Polish carrier **LOT (Polskie Linie Lotnicze)**. The Warsaw-based airline currently has an all western-built fleet. This aircraft was withdrawn in December 1992, sold on to Azerbaijan and later a Bulgarian airline.

Before the peaceful split into the Czech and Slovak Republics the airline for the old Czechoslovakia was CSA (Ceskoslovenske Aerolinie). Pictured at London-Heathrow in May 1988 is Tupolev Tu-154M OK-TCB (c/n 770). The carrier is now known as CSA Czech Airlines. This aircraft was sold to an airline in China.

The Ilyushin IL-62 was a long-range 186-seat airliner with four rear-mounted Kuznetsov NK-8 turbofans of 23,150lb static thrust. First flown in January 1961, the type served in the fleets of many communist states. Pictured at Bangkok in November 1989 is IL-62 OK-GBH (c/n 62404) of CSA. This aircraft is now preserved at the Magic Jet Bar and Restaurant in Heidenreichstein, Austria.

The Ilyushin IL-62M had extra seating and fuel tanks together with more powerful Soloviev D-30KU turbofans giving a higher gross take-off weight. Pictured at Paris-Orly in May 1983 is IL-62M CU-T1218 (c/n 2035657) of Havana-based Cubana de Aviacion SA. It is not surprising that the carrier still operates a mostly Russian-built fleet. This aircraft was withdrawn from use and reported to have been broken up during 2001.

The IL-18 turboprop had a far longer front-line service life than its western counterparts, the Bristol Britannia and the Lockheed Electra. In the west passengers wanted pure jets and got them, whilst in the Soviet Union and other communist states passengers got what they were given. Choice was not a word in Aeroflot's lexicon. The IL-18 had first flown in July 1957 with power from either four Ivchenko A1-20 turboprops of 3755shp or Kuznetsov NK-4s of 4000shp. Pictured at Manchester-Ringway in May 1989 is IL-18V YR-IMF (c/n 184007105) of Romanian carrier Tarom. Sold to Kazakhstan, now stored in Moscow.

Pictured at Abbotsford, British Columbia in August 1986 is Antonov An-74 CCCP-58642 (c/n unknown – line number 02-02) in the livery of Aeroflot. During this time all civil aircraft, from intercontinental airliners to agricultural spray aircraft, were operated by the various divisions of Aeroflot. The An-74 was a STOL medium-capacity, jet-powered aircraft with the engines mounted upon the high wings. It had been developed from the An-72 for polar operations and first flew in 1983. The aircraft was being operated by the Antonov OKB (Design Bureau) and is now in store at their Gostomel plant in the Ukraine.

The An-124 is one of the largest freight aircraft in service anywhere in the world. First flown in December 1982 it was powered by four Lotarev D-18T turbofans with 51,590lbst. This powerplant was the first large turbofan in Russia. Its maximum take-off weight is over 400 tons. Seen at Abbottsford, British Columbia in August 1986 is An-124 Ruslan CCCP-82005 (c/n 4516003) in Aeroflot markings. This aircraft transferred to the Russian Air Force and crashed at Irkutsk in December 1997.

Perhaps the most famous airliner of all time, the BAC/Aerospatiale Concorde was a fine example of advanced technology and flew its passengers at heights and speeds that may never be matched again. Pictured at Miami in June 1989 is Concorde 102 G-BOAF (c/n 216) of British Airways. The carrier phased out the fleet in October 2003. This aircraft made the last-ever flight of the type when, on 26 November 2003, it flew to its birthplace at Filton for preservation by the Bristol Aero Collection.

The quest to find a replacement for the Douglas DC-3 has taxed the brains of many an aeronautical engineer across the world. Most of the designs of the 1950s came into service in the 1960s and by the decade of the 1980s were beginning to need replacement. As for the DC-3, it still flies today. The NAMC (Nihon Aircraft Manufacturing Company) of Japan first flew the YS-11 in 1962. It remains the only post-war Japanese-designed and built airliner. Like many similar designs of the period it was powered by a pair of Rolls-Royce Dart turboprops. Including the prototypes, 182 airframes were constructed and the type was sold worldwide. Pictured at Indianapolis, Indiana in July 1986 is YS-11A N112MP (c/n 2105) of Mid-Pacific Air. The carrier, then Honolulu-based, operated both passenger and freight aircraft. Operations moved to the mainland at the end of the 1980s and all services were suspended in 1995. This freighter is in store at Oakland, California.

Another DC-3 replacement was the Handley Page Herald. The original powerplants were four 870hp Alvis Leonides radial pistons but these were replaced with a pair of Rolls-Royce Darts. It first flew, in this form, as the 'Dart Herald' in March 1958. The design was the least successful, in sales terms, of its rivals with just fifty aircraft being constructed. Pictured at Luton in July 1988 is HPR.7 Herald 214 G-BAVX (c/n 194) of British Air Ferries. The carrier was perhaps more famous for its car-transporting role across the English Channel. Passenger services were also operated and in April 1993 they were renamed British World. At the end of 1992 this aircraft was withdrawn from use at Exeter and then broken up.

Trieste, Italy-based Aligiulia operated scheduled passenger services until flights ceased in 1986. Pictured in store at East Midlands-Castle Donington in June 1986 is HPR.7 Herald 209 I-ZERD (c/n 197). This aircraft was the last Herald built; it was withdrawn from service at Bournemouth at the end of 1996 and broken up the following year.

Pictured at Liverpool-Speke in April 1983 is HPR.7 Herald 401 G-BEYK (c/n 187) of British independent airline Air UK, which flew both domestic and regional international services. The Dutch flag carrier KLM had a share in the company and this grew to a level were they totally owned the airline; they then changed its name to KLM.UK. This aircraft was withdrawn from use at Southend in 1998 and then broken up.

The most successful of the British 'DC-3 replacements' was the Avro (HS) 748. First flown in June 1960 it was, like its competitors, powered by a pair of Rolls-Royce Dart turboprops. As well as UK production it was built under licence by Hindustan in India. Pictured at Seattle-Tacoma, Washington in September 1984 is Avro (Hawker Siddeley) 748 Srs.2B N118CA (c/n 1789) of Cascade Airways. The regional passenger carrier suspended operations in August of the following year while this airframe crashed in Canada in 1988.

Dublin-based Ryanair are now one of the leaders of the low-cost, no-frills airlines of the world with a fleet of over 100 Boeing 737s and plans for many more. They started services in 1985 and operated a number of types before they fixed upon their one-type policy. Pictured at Luton in July 1988 is Avro (HS) 748 Srs.1-106 EI-BSE (c/n 1549). This aircraft was sold on and damaged beyond economic repair in a landing accident in Nepal in 1997.

Based at Oshawa, Ontario, Canadian local service operator Inter City Airways flew for only a couple of years before suspending operation in October 1986. Pictured at base in July of that year is Avro (HS) 748 Srs.2-244 C-GLTC (c/n 1656). This aircraft has been converted to a flying tanker, delivering fuel to remote parts of Canada.

Dutch manufacturer Fokker produced the most successful of all the 'DC-3 replacements' with the F.27 Friendship. It was first flown in 1955 and entered service with Aer Lingus in 1958. Power for the type was again the Rolls-Royce Dart. Pictured at Minneapolis-St Paul in August 1986 is Fokker F.27-500 N271FA (c/n 10434) of based Northwest Orient Airlink. This was the commuter arm of the main carrier. At that time it still had the word 'Orient' in the title, stemming from the fact that many mainline services were operated to that part of the world – the word has now been dropped. The pictured aircraft was sold on to a German company, withdrawn in 2002, and broken up at Baden Baden at the end of 2004.

Pictured at Oshkosh, Wisconsin, in August 1986, is Fokker F.27 Friendship 500 N504AW (c/n 10677) of Appleton-based Air Wisconsin. The airline now operates as a franchise carrier for US Airways Express with its fleet in their livery. This aircraft was sold on, converted to a freighter, and operates for one of the USA's giant parcel companies.

Once the second carrier of Australia, Ansett Airlines was Melbourne-based. It was founded in 1937 and finally suspended operations in 2002. Pictured at base in September 1981 is F.27 Friendship 200 VH-MMS (c/n 10139). Sold on in South America, it was withdrawn from use and is in store in Colombia. (Bob O'Brien)

The Friendship was licence-built in the USA by Fairchild. The first prototype flew from Hagerstown, Maryland in April 1958. Fairchild also developed a stretched version with an extra 6ft 6in (1.98m), which seated up to fifty-six passengers. Pictured at Liverpool-Speke in April 1982 is Fairchild FH-227B Friendship F-GCLP (c/n 564) of French carrier TAT – Touraine Air Transport. The company was merged into Air Liberté in October 1997 and this aircraft was sold on and damaged beyond economic repair in Iceland in July 1998.

Pictured at Miami in June 1989 is Fairchild FH-227C N374RD (c/n 504) of based Airlift International. This carrier, best known as a cargo carrier, operated a small fleet of Friendships in passenger mode. Operations were suspended in 1992 and this aircraft was withdrawn from use at base and broken up the following year.

So successful was the F.27 that Fokker produced a new updated version. First flown in December 1985, the Fokker 50 was now powered by a pair of Pratt & Whitney PW124 2150shp turboprops driving six-bladed propellers. A longer fuselage and new 'glass' cockpit instruments were other improvements. Pictured at Birmingham-Elmdon in May 1989 is Fokker 50 OY-MMU (c/n 20153) of locally based Birmingham European Airways. This aircraft was on lease from Danish carrier Maersk, hence its registration and livery. The company was merged into Brymon in November 1992 and this aircraft now serves with an airline in Latvia.

One of the most successful airliner ranges was that produced by Convair. Production started with the 240 (2 engines, 40 passengers). This first flew in March 1947 and was powered by a pair of 2400hp P&W R-2800 radial piston engines. Pictured at Tucson, Arizona in September 1988 is Convair CV-240 N152PA (c/n 279) of San Juan, Puerto Rico-based cargo carrier Sundance Airlines. The company suspended operations in 1989. This aircraft was sold on to a Canadian operator. Although it is current there, it has been acquired as a source of engines for another operator's Canadair CL-215.

Convair stretched the 240 by a total of 4ft 6in (1.37m) to make the 340. It first flew in October 1951 and could seat an extra four passengers. Pictured at Nassau, Bahamas in August 1980 is Convair CV-340 N920RC (c/n 118) of St Petersburg, Florida-based Red Carpet Airlines, by then converted to a CV-440 having a lengthened nose radar and longer engine nacelles. This general charter operator changed its name to Aerosun International in August 1981 and this aircraft was sold to a company in the Dominican Republic where it is currently in store. (Bob O'Brien)

Pictured at Oshkosh, Wisconsin in August 1986 is Convair CV-440 (converted from CV-340) N29DR (c/n 146) of **Combs Freightair**. This Denver-based cargo carrier ceased operations in May 1985 and this aircraft is still in store at this location.

So good was the basic Convair airframe that turboprop power was added to convert many to CV-580s. Pac-Aero replaced the pistons with a pair of Allison 501 3750shp turboprops. Pictured in store at Tucson, Arizona in September 1988 is Convair CV-580 N5822 (c/n 54) in the livery of **Atlantic Gulf Airlines** of Miami. The carrier moved to various sites in Florida and had become Ocean Air in 1986. This aircraft was broken up for spare parts in 2002.

Pictured at Philadelphia in January 1987 is Convair CV-580 N511GA (c/n 39) of Louisiana-based Gulf Air. The carrier was renamed Transocean Airways in 1989 and this aircraft is currently operated in South Africa. (Bob O'Brien)

Tucson, Arizona-based Sierra Pacific Airlines has been operating since 1976, today flying a pair of Boeing 737s. Pictured under maintenance at Marana, Arizona in October 1984 is Convair CV-580 N73153 (c/n 179). This aircraft has been converted to an airborne fire engine and is operated in Canada as a water bomber to put out forest fires.

Based in London, Ontario, **Air Ontario** was an affiliate of Air Canada that was later absorbed into the main company. Pictured at Toronto in July 1986 is Convair CV-580 C-GQHA (c/n 147). This aircraft was sold to a Spanish freight company, withdrawn and stored.

Oslo, Norway-based **Nor Fly Charter** operated three Convairs on ad-hoc charter services. Pictured at Liverpool-Speke in April 1984, bringing in a football team, is Convair CV-580 LN-BWG (c/ 42). The carrier merged into Partnair in January 1985 and this aircraft currently flies as a freighter in New Zealand.

As an alternative to the Allison turboprops some Convair CV-240s were re-engined with Rolls-Royce Darts, these being redesignated CV-600s. Pictured on the move at Boston in August 1986 is Convair CV-600 N94208 (c/n 15) of Bangor, Maine-based **Bar Harbor Airlines**. The carrier suspended services in January 1991 and this aircraft was withdrawn from use in 1989 in Texas and broken up.

The sole postwar airliners from the Glen L Martin Company were the Martin 2-0-2 and 4-0-4 twin-engined aircraft. Direct competitors of the piston Convair liners they were outsold by a large margin. From the 2-0-2 came the 4-0-4, now pressurised but with the same P&W R-2800 radial piston engines. Pictured at Miami in August 1986 is Martin 4-0-4 N258S (c/n 14232), still in the livery of Florida Airlines. This company had ceased scheduled operations in January 1980 but resumed them under Chapter 11 bankruptcy protection. In August 1981 they became Southern International Airways. This aircraft was broken up at Miami at the end of 1988.

Air Florida was one of the carriers that expanded under the 1978 deregulation of the US airline system. Before they ceased all services and merged with Midway Express in July 1984 they had operated aircraft as large as the DC-10. Pictured at its Miami base in October 1981 is Martin 4-0-4 N259S (c/n 14233). This airframe has been preserved at the Glenn L Martin Aviation Museum.

First flown in July 1948 and powered by four Rolls-Royce Dart turboprops, the Vickers Viscount became the most successful airliner of its generation. It was sold and operated worldwide. Pictured at Liverpool-Speke in April 1987 is Viscount 802 G-AOHM (c/n 162) of British Air Ferries. Sold on to an operator in Africa it was damaged beyond economic repair whilst attempting to take off in Chad in 2001.

Pictured at Liverpool-Speke in August 1984 is Viscount 836 G-BFZL (c/n 435) of British Midland Airways. This scheduled UK-based passenger carrier now operates services, both domestic and international, with a fleet of mostly Airbus designs under the name bmi. This aircraft was one of the last Viscounts in service when it was damaged beyond economic repair whilst attempting to take off in the Congo in 2003.

Pictured at its Tucson, Arizona base in September 1988 is Viscount 745D N180RC (c/n 51) of Go Air. This carrier specialised in leasing its VIP-equipped aircraft to rock groups for their tours. In 1987 the company had been sold to Jadepoint and this aircraft was broken up at this location in 1993.

Under the management of its head Richard Branson (now Sir), Virgin Airways has grown in both size and public awareness since its start in 1984. Pictured landing at London-Gatwick in July 1988 is Viscount 806 G-AOYP (c/n 265). This aircraft operated a service to Maastricht in Holland. The airline, now known as Virgin Atlantic, only operates four-engined long-haul types today. This Viscount was sold in Africa and reduced to spare parts at Lanseria.

The follow on to the Viscount was the Vanguard. This was a short to medium range airliner seating up to 139 passengers. Power was supplied by four Rolls-Royce Tyne turboprops of 5545shp. It first flew in January 1959 but the production run was just forty-four aircraft including the prototype. By the end of the 1980s most left flying were in the role of freighters, these being conversions to Merchantman configuration. Pictured at Liverpool-Speke in April 1984 is V.953C Vanguard/Merchantman G-APEK (c/n 714) of Air Bridge, a cargo carrier based at East Midlands. They were renamed Hunting Cargo Airlines in September 1992 while this aircraft was withdrawn from use in France in 1989 and scrapped the following year.

Based upon the Bristol Britannia, the Canadair CL-44 was a freighter with a swing-tail for easy loading. The airframe had been stretched and the power came from four Rolls-Royce Tyne turboprops. This variant first flew in November 1960 and total production, including the CC-106 Yukon – a side cargo door version for the RCAF, was just thirty-nine aircraft. Pictured at Miami in October 1981 is CL-44D4-1 HC-BHS (c/n 14) of Aeca (Aeroservicios Ecuatorianos CA). The Guayaquil-based cargo carrier suspended operations in 2000. This aircraft was damaged beyond repair at Miami in January 1982 and broken up.

Pictured at Luton in September 1983 is Canadair CL-44D4-2 G-BRED (c/n 37) of based Redcoat Cargo Airlines. The carrier had ceased trading in May of the previous year and this airframe was sold on and damaged beyond economic repair in the Congo, following an explosion in 2000.

Production of the Lockheed C-130 Hercules began in 1954 and continues to this day with the C-130J model. No other aircraft can have had such a long unbroken run. The majority of the aircraft are for the air forces of the world but a small number of civil variants have been produced. Pictured at East Midlands-Castle Donington in June 1988 is Lockheed L-100-30 Hercules HB-ILG (c/n 4698) of Zurich-based Zimex Aviation. This company operates in many locations, especially in Africa. This aircraft currently serves with an American cargo carrier in Alaska.

Pictured at its Miami base in August 1986 is Lockheed L-100-30 Hercules N520SJ (c/n 4299) of Southern Air Transport. This was an all-cargo carrier that operated worldwide. Operations were suspended in September 1998 and this aircraft was withdrawn from use.

The Bristol 170 Freighter was most famous for its carriage of cars across the English Channel. It was, however, an all-purpose cargo carrier with two clamshell doors in the nose to facilitate loading. Examples served in all parts of the world and its simple fixed undercarriage could handle unprepared or grass strips. Pictured at Auckland-Ardmore, New Zealand in March 1985 is Bristol B.170 Mk.31M ZK-EPF (c/n 13134) in the livery of Hercules Airlines. This was a suitable name for a carrier, who sold its last aircraft in 1989, as the power plants of the aircraft were a pair of 1980hp Bristol Hercules 734 radial piston engines. Bristol was one of the few airframe manufactures who also built their own engines. This aircraft was sold on to a Canadian company and crashed on landing in British Columbia in 1988. (Bob O'Brien)

Pictured in store at Melbourne-Essendon, in June 1983, is Bristol B.170 Mk.31M VH-ADL (c/n 13193) in the colours of Air Express, a locally based cargo airline. The company had suspended operations in 1979 and this aircraft has been preserved at a museum in Victoria. (Bob O'Brien)

Pictured at Stansted, in July 1982, is Bristol B.170 Freighter Mk.31 G-BISU (c/n 13218) of **Instone Airlines**. This carrier, which specialised in the transport of racehorses, was the last commercial operator of the type in the UK. It ceased operations in 1984 and this aircraft was sold in Canada. It was later returned to the UK for flying preservation but was damaged beyond repair whilst taking off in July 1996.

The Armstrong-Whitworth Argosy was a large bulk capacity freighter. It had a high wing, twin booms, and the civil variants had both front and rear loading doors. Power was from four Rolls-Royce Dart turboprops. The first flight was in 1959. Pictured at Liverpool-Speke in May 1981 is Argosy 101 G-BEOZ (c/n 6660) of **Air Bridge Carriers**. Based at East Midlands, their role at Liverpool was the transportation of newspapers. In 1993 they were renamed Hunting Cargo Airlines and this aircraft has been preserved at East Midlands Airport.

The Lockheed Electra first flew in 1957; it was powered by four 3750shp Allison 501 turboprops. Its entry into service coincided with the arrival of the early jets and the public did not want anything with propellers. Hence its front-line service with major carriers was relatively short but the design has given long service to smaller airlines and cargo companies. Pictured at Rio de Janeiro, in June 1989, is L-188A Electra PP-VNK (c/n 1040) of Brazilian carrier Varig (Viacao Aerea Rio-Grandense SA). This airline, which today has an all-jet fleet, was the pioneer of the 'Ponte Aerea' or Air Bridge shuttle between Rio de Janeiro and Sao Paulo. This was the first of such services, now popular, of high-frequency flights between major cities. The pictured aircraft was converted to a water-bomber role in Canada and crashed in British Columbia during 2003. (Bob O'Brien)

Keflavik-based Eagle Air of Iceland operated a mixed fleet of passenger and cargo aircraft. They ceased operations in 1990. Pictured at Rotterdam in June 1983 is Lockheed L-188A Electra TF-VLN (c/n 1096) in cargo configuration. This aircraft was sold on, withdrawn from service, and broken up in Aruba in 1990.

Pictured at Toronto in July 1986 is L-188CF Electra C-GNWC (c/n 2015) of Northwest Territorial Airways. This carrier was based at Yellowknife, in the far north of Canada, and operated a regular nightly cargo service. It was renamed NWT Air in 1989; this aircraft was sold on and operated in the UK before being broken up for spares in 1998.

Pictured climbing out of Miami in October 1981 is L-188CF Electra HR-TNL (c/n 1134) of TAN (Transportes Aereos Nacionales). This airline was the flag carrier for the Central American republic of Honduras. In 1991 the company merged and adopted the name SAHSA while this aircraft crashed in Honduras in 1990.

The tramp steamer of the skies, the Curtiss C-46 Commando has the same layout as the DC-3 but is a much larger machine. It can now only be found in a few countries of South America, the northern parts of Canada, or Alaska. Pictured departing Miami in October 1981 is C-46 Commando N5370N (c/n 22601) of Rich International Airways. Locally based, they flew cargo and later passenger charters before suspending services in 1997.This aircraft was sold in Nicaragua and was reported to have crashed there in 1994.

Pictured at Opa Locka, Florida in October 1981 is Curtiss C-46D Commando CC-CDC (c/n 30653) of Santiago, Chile-based Linea Aerea Sud-Americana. This cargo carrier ceased operations in 1982 and the aircraft has been preserved at Warner Robins Air Force Base in Georgia.

Seen at Miami in March 1981 is C-46A Commando HH-AHA (c/n 26496) of Air Haiti. The carrier, which was later banned from operations to the USA because of concerns about safety standards, would lease US-registered freighters to operate their services. They renamed themselves Air Adeah in 2001 and this aircraft is in store, in a derelict condition, in the capital Port-au-Prince. (Bob O'Brien)

The sale of surplus military Lockheed Super Constellations from the USAF and US Navy gave a number of operators, in the 1980s, an excellent freight aircraft at low acquisition costs. Pictured at Arlington, Washington in September 1984 is L-1049 Super Constellation N4247K (c/n 4144) of **Winky's Fish**. This company planned to haul salmon from Alaska to the 'lower 48' states of America. This aircraft has been in store in Manila, Philippines, following a failed business attempt to fly fresh tuna fish from Palau Island in the Pacific Ocean to Nagoya, Japan in 1987. Only a small number of flights were possible before the venture ceased.

The Dominican Republic was a hotbed of Constellation operations during the 1980s. Pictured landing at Miami in June 1989 is Lockheed L-1049F Super Constellation HI-515CT (c/n 4192) of **AMSA (Aerolineas Mundo SA)**. Based in the capital, Santo Domingo, the cargo carrier suspended services in 1997. This aircraft crashed into the sea off Puerto Rico in April 1990.

Pictured landing at Miami in June 1989 is L-1049F Super Constellation HI-548CT (c/n 4202) of Dominican cargo carrier **Aerochago**. This company finally suspended operations in 2004 having for some years just leased cargo aircraft from US-based airlines. This aircraft was broken up during 2000.

It is unlikely that any decade of aviation, for many years to come, will not feature the Douglas DC-3. If ever there was an aeroplane that will go on and on it is this one. Pictured on the move at Boston in August 1986, is DC-3 Dakota N43PB (c/n 1953) of PBA (Provincetown Boston Airlines). This passenger carrier had a summer base in Hyannis, Massachusetts and in the winter moved its operations to Naples, Florida. In September 1988 the company was taken over by Bar Harbor Airlines. This aircraft was exported to Mexico and has been reported as withdrawn from use at Hautulco.

Pictured at Fairford in July 1985 is Douglas DC-3 F-GDPP (c/n 9172) of French line Transvalair – Air Charter Express. The Caen-based company operated freight and later passenger services before operations were suspended in 1994. This aircraft has been preserved in flying condition at La Ferté Alais.

Pictured at its St John's, Antigua base in June 1983 is Douglas DC-3 V2-LIX (c/n 25623) of **Seagreen Air Transport**. The company flew scheduled cargo flights around the Leeward Islands and other Caribbean destinations. Operations were suspended in 1985 and this aircraft sold in America. It is reportedly derelict at Opa Locka, Florida but unconfirmed. (Bob O'Brien)

Pictured at Antigua in June 1983 is Douglas DC-3 VP-LVJ (c/n 9795) of **Air BVI**. This was the airline of the British Virgin Islands, a UK colony. It suspended operations in June 1991 and this aircraft was destroyed by Hurricane Hugo whilst in store at Puerto Rico in 1989. (Bob O'Brien)

Pictured landing at Miami in June 1989 is Douglas DC-3 N2685W (c/n 33010) of **B Airways**. The carrier with the shortest name suspended operations the following year. This aircraft was sold to Basler for conversion to turboprop power and has since joined the Royal Thai Air Force.

Classic Air of Zurich operated two DC-3s for pleasure and sightseeing flights. Pictured at base, in August 1987, is Douglas DC-3 HB-ISC (c/n 9995). The carrier suspended operations in 1995 and this aircraft is to be found, in old Swissair colours, operated by JU-Air doing the same job.

Following release by the US Navy a number of surplus C-117 Super Dakotas came onto the market. Pictured at Detroit-Willow Run in July 1986 is Douglas C-117D N873SN (c/n 43327) of based Intercoastal Airways. In 1989 the company sold its aircraft. This one went to the Philippines where it was damaged beyond economic repair in August 1999.

Millardair of Toronto was another operator of the tall-tailed Super Dakota. Pictured at base in July 1986 is Douglas C-117D C-GDIK (c/n 43369). The carrier suspended operations in June 1990 and this aircraft was sold to America and is currently believed to have been withdrawn from use.

The big three Douglas four-engined piston-powered transports – the DC-4, DC-6 and DC-7 – could all be found in reasonable numbers during the 1980s, but all in a slow decline of operational aircraft. Pictured at Chandler, Arizona in October 1984, on lease from Biegert Aviation, is Douglas DC-4 Skymaster N44909 (c/n 27371) in the livery of Seafood Resources International. The interior had been fitted out for fish transport from Alaska. Sold on, the aircraft was converted to a flying fuel tanker and crashed while landing in British Columbia in 1997.

Pictured in store at Chandler, Arizona in September 1988 is Douglas DC-4 Skymaster N301JT (c/n 18375) in the colours of Honolulu-based Pacific Air Express. This carrier had operated a freight service around the Hawaiian Islands until August 1986 when services were suspended. This aircraft was scrapped at this location in February 2006.

Pictured just before touchdown at Miami in August 1986 is Douglas DC-4 Skymaster N97810 (c/n 10522). Owned by World Wide Inc. it carries the titles Air Ays. This aircraft is believed to be withdrawn from use at Opa Locka, Florida.

Miami-based **Aerial Transit** operated freight services to many locations in the Caribbean. Pictured landing at base in June 1989 is Douglas DC-6A N96BL (c/n 43574). The company was sold and renamed Southeast Cargo Airlines in February 1994 and this aircraft was sold. It is believed to have been withdrawn from use at Miami and scrapped.

Based in Santo Domingo, Dominican carrier **APA International Air** leased this Douglas DC-6BF N95BL (c/n 45220) from US company Bellomy-Lawson. They operated until 2001. This aircraft, pictured at Miami in June 1989, was withdrawn from use, stored and is believed to have been scrapped.

Pictured landing at its Miami base in June 1989 is Douglas DC-6BF N841TA (c/n 44891) of **Trans-Air-Link**. This was one of the companies who operated general cargo services around the Caribbean. The airline flew until 2003 but by then using turboprop aircraft. This airframe has been preserved in *'The 1940 Air Terminal Museum'* at Houston-Hobby Airport, Texas.

A renowned tax haven, the UK colony of the Cayman Islands has as its main carrier **Cayman Airways**. Pictured operating a cargo service to Miami in October 1981 is Douglas DC-6A N61267 (c/n 45374). This aircraft was withdrawn and stored in Puerto Rico and damaged beyond repair following Hurricane George in September 1998.

With its Detroit-Willow Run base, **Trans Continental Airlines** specialised in freight services for the local motor industry. Pictured there in July 1986 is Douglas DC-6A N515TY (c/n 44175). In March 2000 the carrier was renamed Express.net Airlines. This aircraft had been sold to a company in Africa, and was broken up in 1997.

A very low number of the largest of the Douglas pistons, the DC-7, was still active by the 1980s. Pictured at its Miami base is Douglas DC-7CF N869TA (c/n 45188) of Trans-Air-Link. This aircraft was sold to an African operator and later withdrawn from use in the Congo.

Powered by three tail-mounted Rolls-Royce Spey turbofans, the DH (HS) Trident first flew in January 1962. The aircraft had been tailored to the needs of launch customer BEA and it therefore lacked the flexibility to sell in large numbers: 117 being the total production run. The final variant, the Trident 3, had an extra R-R RB.162 engine fitted to boost take-off capability. Pictured at Manchester-Ringway in October 1982 is HS.121 Trident 3B G-AWZM (c/n 2314) in British Airways markings. This aircraft has been preserved by the Science Museum at Wroughton.

The Fokker Fellowship was a short-haul airliner with an original capacity of sixty-five seats; first flown in May 1967 it was powered by a pair of tail-mounted Rolls-Royce Spey turbofans. Pictured at Minneapolis-St Paul in July 1986 is Fokker F.28 Fellowship 1000 C-GTEO (c/n 11991) of Norcanair. Based in Saskatoon, Saskatchewan, the carrier merged into Time Air at the start of 1988. This aircraft is currently in store at Saskatoon.

Based in North Carolina, Piedmont Airlines was one of the growth success carriers following deregulation. Pictured at Miami in June 1989 is Fokker F.28 Fellowship 1000 N467US (c/n 11087). The carrier became US Air and this aircraft was sold to a Peruvian airline and is currently in store at Lima.

The F.28 was stretched by 7ft 3in (2.2m) to give a seating capacity of seventy-nine. This variant, the 2000, first flew in April 1971. Pictured at Zurich in August 1987 is F.28 Fellowship 2000 F-GDUS (c/n 11053) of TAT (Transport Aerien Transregional). The name had been changed in 1984 but keeping the same initials. In 1997 it merged into Air Liberté. This aircraft was withdrawn from use at Paris-CDG in 2001 and used by the fire service for training.

The Fellowship 3000 had the short body of the 1000 with the extended wings and other improvements of the 4000. Pictured at Zurich in August 1987 is F.28 Fellowship 3000 OO-DJA (c/n 11163) of DAT-Belgian Regional Airlines. They were a subsidiary of SABENA, the national flag carrier. DAT was derived from Delta Air Transport. Following the demise of the parent company in November 2001 the company became known as SN Brussels Airlines. This aircraft was sold on to Canada and is currently in store at Calgary.

Pictured at Nairobi in August 1980 is F.28 Fellowship 3000 3D-ALN (c/n 11136) of Royal Swazi National Airlines. The carrier suspended operations in April 1999 and this aircraft was sold in South Africa where it is currently in store at Lanseria. (Bob O'Brien)

The best-selling variant of the Fellowship was the 4000. This had the longer fuselage of the 2000, increased wingspan and more powerful Rolls-Royce Speys. Pictured at Bangkok in November 1989 is F.28 Fellowship 4000 XY-AGA (c/n 11232) of Myanma Airways. This is the national airline for the country that used to be known as Burma. It operates only limited international flights and this aircraft is still operational with them.

The BAe 146 was a short- to medium-haul airliner with four Avco-Lycoming ALF-502 turbofans mounted under its high wing. It first flew in September 1981 and was renowned for its very low noise footprint. It came in three fuselage lengths: the 100, 200 and 300 series. Pictured at Orange County, California in September 1988 is BAe 146-200A N177US (c/n E2039) of US Air. This airport had introduced very strict noise restrictions and the 146 was always well within them. The carrier is now known as US Airways and this aircraft is currently operated by an Irish airline.

Pictured in September 1988 at Los Angeles-LAX is BAe 146-200A N146AC (c/n E2057) in the hybrid colours of AirCal and American Airlines. AirCal had been bought by American in 1987 but had not yet put the aircraft into their full livery. This aircraft was sold to a UK company and is currently in store at Exeter.

Another hybrid, pictured at Manchester-Ringway in April 1989, is BAe 146-200A N408XV (c/n E2077) of US carrier Presidential Airways on lease to British Airways. This Washington DC-based company had set up in 1985 to offer high frequencies, low fares and yet supply a full service. Operations were suspended at the end of 1989 and this aircraft is currently in service with a German company.

San Diego-based PSA (Pacific Southwest Airlines) offered high-frequency flights and low fares along the Pacific coast and adjoining states. Pictured at Los Angeles-LAX in August 1986 is BAe 146-200A N354PS (c/n E2034). In 1988 PSA was merged into US Air and this aircraft was sold in the Philippines and written off after it overran the runway at Catarman in November 2005.

Pictured in November 1989 at its Bangkok base is BAe 146-300 HS-TBL (c/n E3131) of Thai International, the nation's flag carrier. This aircraft is currently operated by an airline in Bulgaria.

To replace the Viscount, BAC designed a short- to medium-haul airliner, the One-Eleven. It first flew in August 1963 and was powered by a pair of Rolls-Royce Spey turbofans. It became one of the most successful British airliners and sold well in the very competitive and protectionist American market. Pictured at Manchester-Ringway in October 1982 is One-Eleven 518FG G-BCWA (c/n 205) of UK independent Dan-Air. The carrier was taken over by British Airways in November 1992; this aircraft was withdrawn from service that year and then broken up.

BAF (British Air Ferries) BAC One-Eleven 416EK G-SURE (c/n 129) is pictured at Manchester-Ringway in October 1982. The carrier was renamed British World in April 1993, by which time this aircraft had been sold to a Nigerian operator, withdrawn, stored and then broken up in 1992.

Once the second airline of the UK, British Caledonian flew both long- and short-haul services from their Gatwick base. They were taken over by British Airways in 1988. Pictured at Liverpool-Speke in April 1983 is BAC One-Eleven 320AZ G-BKAW (c/n 113). This aircraft spent three years as an attraction at a shopping village in Lancashire before being broken up in 1998.

The national airline of El Salvador, TACA International Airlines has today grown to be the central part of a group operating services for several Central and South American countries. Pictured at Miami in October 1981 is BAC One-Eleven 407AW YS-18C (c/n 106). This aircraft was sold to a Nigerian carrier and is in store at Kano.

British Island Airways had evolved from British United, the name being derived from services to the Isle of Man and the Channel Islands. Pictured at London-Gatwick in July 1987 is BAC One-Eleven 518FG G-AXMG (c/n 201). The airline suspended services in 1990 while this aircraft ended its days in South Africa, being withdrawn in 1998 and broken up in June 2005.

Before settling upon one type of aircraft for the entire fleet, the Boeing 737, Irish low-cost, no-frills carrier **Ryanair** operated a number of other designs. Pictured at Luton in September 1988 is BAC One-Eleven 525FT EI-BSZ (c/n 272). Sold on, this aircraft was broken up in 1996 after being damaged beyond economic repair following a heavy landing at Istanbul the previous year.

British Airways used the One-Eleven for many of its domestic and regional European services. Pictured at Manchester-Ringway in April 1987 is BAC One-Eleven 510ED G-AVMR (c/n 145). It was withdrawn and broken up at Bournemouth in 2001.

Based at Nassau on New Providence Island, **Bahamasair** is the flag carrier for the island chain nation. Services are flown, both domestic and international, in the region. Pictured at base in August 1980 is BAC One-Eleven 401AK C6-BDJ (c/n 089). Sold on, this airframe was withdrawn and stored in Guatemala in 2003. (Bob O'Brien)

In America three four-engine jetliners vied for business from the airlines of the world. The Boeing 707 and the Douglas DC-8 were a great success but the third, the Convair 880, was a commercial failure, with just sixty-five being built, despite being the fastest of the three. Pictured at Miami in October 1981 is Convair 880-22-1 AN-BIB (c/n 22-009) in the livery of Lanica of Nicaragua. The carrier operated the type from 1972 to 1977 and was declared insolvent in March 1981. This aircraft was broken up at the end of 1981.

The French Sud Aviation SE-210 Caravelle was the west's first medium-range passenger jet. It first flew in May 1955 and entered service with SAS in April 1959. Pictured at Sydney-Mascot, Australia in April 1988 is SE-210 Caravelle 10B-3 F-GEPC (c/n 184) of Noumea-based Air Caledonie International. This is a French possession in the Pacific. The airline currently uses the shorter name AirCalin and this aircraft was sold on and crashed in Mexico in 1995. (Bob O'Brien)

A Swiss charter company based in Geneva, CTA (Compagnie de Transport Aerien) was owned by Swissair. Pictured at Zurich in August 1987 is Sud Aviation SE-210 Caravelle 10B HB-ICQ (c/n 222). The airline was merged with Balair to form Balair-CTA, then absorbed into the main company and re-launched again before the final demise of Swissair. This aircraft was sold on, withdrawn from use, and broken up for spare parts in Cyprus during 1991.

Powered by three Rolls-Royce RB.211 turbofans each, with an output of 42,000lb static thrust, the Lockheed TriStar first flew from Palmdale, California in November 1970. Pictured at London-Gatwick in July 1988 is L-1011 TriStar 385 G-BEAL (c/n 1145) of British holiday charter carrier Caledonian Airways. The company had a number of different parents and was eventually merged into JMC Air. This aircraft was sold on, withdrawn and stored at Stansted where it is currently used for training.

Pictured on take-off from Miami in October 1981 is Lockheed L-1011 TriStar 1 N334EA (c/n 1141) of based Eastern Airlines. The carrier had a long history, being formed in 1928 and finally closing down in 1991. This aircraft was converted to a freighter and later withdrawn and stored. Its registration was cancelled in 2004.

Another American carrier with a long history was **TWA – Trans World Airlines**. It dated back to 1930, operating then as Transcontinental and Western. Pictured landing at New York-JFK in May 1989 is L-1011 TriStar 100 N81028 (c/n 1108). TWA were taken over by American Airlines in February 2001. This aircraft was sold to a Canadian airline, withdrawn, stored and broken up at Marana, Arizona.

Pictured landing at Manchester-Ringway in April 1989 is L-1011 TriStar 100 C-FTNL (c/n 1073) of **Air Canada**. This aircraft had its registration cancelled in March 2003 when it was scrapped.

Indianapolis-based **American Trans Air** operates both domestic and international charter flights. Pictured at London-Gatwick in July 1987 is L-1011 TriStar 1 N191AT (c/n 1084). The carrier currently brands itself as ATA and this aircraft was withdrawn and stored at Roswell, New Mexico in 2002.

From its Port of Spain base in the Republic of Trinidad and Tobago BWIA International flew both long- and short-haul services with a fleet ranging from a DHC-8 to an Airbus A340. Pictured at London-Heathrow in May 1988 is L-1011 TriStar 500 N3140D (c/n 1233). In December 2006 the airline ceased all services and was replaced by Caribbean Airlines. This aircraft was sold on, withdrawn, and stored at Marana, Arizona in 2001.

The flag carrier for the nation of Sri Lanka is currently Srilankan Airlines. This name was adopted in July 1999, prior to this they were known as Air Lanka. Pictured at Zurich in August 1987 is L-1011 TriStar 100 4R-ULC (c/n 1053). It was withdrawn in 2000 at the airline's base.

Pictured at Manchester-Ringway in April 1987 is L-1011 TriStar 200 G-BHBO (c/n 1205) of **British Airways**. The type had been ordered by BEA in 1972 and by the time they were delivered, in October 1974, the carrier had been merged with BOAC to form BA. They remained in service until 1992. This aircraft was sold on, converted to a freighter, withdrawn from use, and its registration cancelled in 2001.

Gulf Air was one of the few multi-nation carriers. It operated for the countries of Bahrain, Oman and Abu Dhabi; in 2005 the latter emirate withdrew from the group followed in May 2007 by the Sultanate of Oman leaving the airline 100% owned by the Kingdom of Bahrain. Pictured at London-Heathrow in July 1987 is L-1011 TriStar 200 N92TB (c/n 1203). It was converted to a freighter, used by an American carrier, and is currently in store in North Carolina.

Operated by the holiday charter arm of BA, **British Airtours** Lockheed L-1011 TriStar 1 G-BBAJ (c/n 1106) is pictured at London-Gatwick in July 1987. The aircraft was operated in a high-density, one-class seating arrangement for 393 passengers. Following the takeover of BCal by BA, the company was renamed Caledonian. This aircraft was withdrawn and, following a period of storage, broken up for spares in 2002.

First flown in November 1959 the Boeing 720 was 9ft (2.74m) shorter than the standard 707-100 series. It was designed for short- to medium-haul routes, having a lower fuel capacity. Pictured at London-Gatwick in July 1987 is Boeing 720-047B 9H-AAK (c/n 18063) of Air Malta. The flag carrier for the Mediterranean island republic currently operates a mix of Airbus and Boeing twin-engine, single-aisle aircraft. This airframe, like so many of its type, was used for spares for the USAF KC-135 program and then broken up at Davis Monthan Air Force Base, Arizona.

Bogotá-based Avianca (Aerovias Nacionales de Colombia) is the national flag carrier. Pictured at Miami in October 1981 is Boeing 707-321C HK-1849 (c/n 18766). The airline first used the type, on lease in 1960, to replace the Lockheed Constellation. They brought the 707 into their own fleet in 1976 and operated them until 1991. This aircraft was sold on, converted to a freighter, withdrawn and stored in Uruguay in 1999.

TWA – Trans World Airlines first operated the 707 on US domestic routes in March 1959 and then across the North Atlantic in November of that year. Pictured landing at Miami in October 1981 is Boeing 707-131B N795TW (c/n 18758). This aircraft was withdrawn from service the following year, joined the KC-135 spares program and was broken up at Davis Monthan AFB.

Miami-based Challenge Air Cargo grew from operating Curtiss C-46s to 707s and eventually DC-10s. In 2001 the name was changed to Centurion Air Cargo. Pictured at base in June 1989 is Boeing 707-330C N707HE (c/n 20124). This airframe is currently in store at San Antonio, Texas. Its final role was to test engines.

Santiago, Chile-based LADECO (Linea Aerea del Cobre) operated both passenger and cargo services. Pictured at Miami in June 1989 is Boeing 707-327C CC-CYA (c/n 19530) configured for cargo. The company ceased operations in October 1994. This aircraft was sold on, and operated in Romania, where it is believed to have now been withdrawn from use.

By the 1980s the majority of 707s still in service were configured for cargo operations. Pictured at Miami in June 1989 is Lan Chile Cargo Boeing 707-385C CC-CEB (c/n 19000). Today, the carrier operates in a number of South American countries under the LAN prefix. This aircraft joined the Chilean Air Force and was converted to a Phalcon Airborne Early Warning aircraft, still serving to this day.

A scheduled cargo carrier Tampa (Transporte Aereos Mercantiles Panamericanos) was founded in 1973 and from its base in Medellin, Colombia flies international services currently with DC-8 and Boeing 767 aircraft. Pictured at Miami in June 1989 is Boeing 707-321C HK-3333X (c/n 18714). This airframe was withdrawn, stored and then broken up at the end of 2000.

South African carrier Safair currently operates a wide mix of both passenger and freight aircraft from its Johannesburg base. Pictured at Cape Town in May 1986 is Boeing 707-344C ZS-LSF (c/n 20283). This aircraft later joined the South African Air Force and currently serves in a communications intelligence role. (Bob O'Brien)

Formed in 1983, Florida West flew scheduled and charter cargo services around the region from its base at Miami. Pictured here in June 1989 is Boeing 707-321C N710FW (c/n 20017). The carrier currently operates a single Boeing 767 and the pictured aircraft is in service with a Brazilian cargo airline.

Quito-based Ecuatoriana was formed in 1974 as the flag carrier for Ecuador. Both passenger and cargo services were flown by aircraft in their very attractive livery. Pictured at Miami in June 1989 is Boeing 707-321B HC-BHY (c/n 20033). The airline was taken over by VASP of Brazil but suspended services in 2002. This aircraft was reduced to spares at the company base in 1996.

Formed in 1984 in Ouagadougou, Burkina Faso, Naganagani Compagnie Nationale operated its passenger and cargo services for just eight years before suspending operations. Pictured at Manchester-Ringway in May 1989 is Boeing 707-328C XT-BBF (c/n 19521) operating a sub-lease for a holiday charter flight. This aircraft was sold on to a number of operators before being damaged beyond economic repair after an aborted take-off at Bratislava in February 1999.

First flown in February 1963 the Boeing 727 was a medium-range airliner powered by three rear-mounted P&W JT-8D turbojets. It was at one time the best-selling jet airliner in the world with sales of 1832 aircraft; this figure has long since been passed by both the 737 and the Airbus A320. Pictured at Miami in June 1989 is Boeing 727-95 HC-BJL (c/n 19596) of SAETA (Sociedad Anonima Ecuatoriana de Transportes Aereos). Quito-based, they flew scheduled passenger services in South, Central and North America. The carrier suspended operations in 2000 and this aircraft was withdrawn and stored at Latacunga-Cotopaxi.

Pictured at Miami in October 1981 is Boeing 727-46 HP-661 (c/n 19280) of Air Panama. This company suspended operations during 1990 and this aircraft was sold to a carrier in Colombia, withdrawn and then broken up in 1996.

Aviateca (Aerolineas de Guatemala) Boeing 727-25C TG-ALA (c/n 19302) is pictured at Miami in June 1989. The Central American carrier is now part of the TACA group of airlines. This aircraft has since been fitted with Rolls-Royce Tay engines and currently operates as a 727-25C (QF) – 'Quiet Freighter' for a major US parcel carrier.

Emery Worldwide was once one of the giants of US parcel delivery operations. Pictured at Omaha, Nebraska in July 1986 is Boeing 727-51C N415EX (c/n 18945). The carrier suspended operations in August 2001 and this aircraft, like the one pictured above, has been re-engined and operates for the same company.

Federal Express have grown to such a size and become such a well-known company that they have shortened their name to just FedEx. They fly several hundred aircraft from Cessna Caravans to MD-11s. Pictured at Omaha, Nebraska in July 1986 is Boeing 727-25C N118FE (c/n 19300). This aircraft was withdrawn in 2002 and broken up for spares.

Pictured at New York-JFK in May 1989 is Boeing 727-51 N29KA (c/n 18803) of Las Vegas-based Key Air. The carrier suspended services in May 1993 and this aircraft was withdrawn and is in store at Greenwood-Le Flore, Mississippi.

Earlier in this aircraft's life it had been involved in the still unsolved mystery of D B Cooper. In November 1971 the aircraft was owned by Northwest Orient and operating service NW305 from Minneapolis to Reno via Great Falls, Missoula, Spokane, Portland and Seattle. On the Portland to Seattle sector it was hijacked. Landing at Seattle, the passengers were released and the aircraft refuelled for a journey to Mexico. Whilst on this next sector the hijacker, who had collected four parachutes and $200,000 in cash, ordered the pilot to depressurise the aircraft and lower the undercarriage, thus ensuring the maximum flying speed of 190 mph. He then opened the under-fuselage entrance door and bailed out. He has never been seen to this day, albeit some of the money was found in a remote area. Following a spate of copy-cat hijackings a modification was made to the aft-stairs to stop them opening in flight; it was named the 'Cooper vane'.

Today one of the world's largest carriers, United Airlines has a history dating back to 1931. Pictured at Dayton, Ohio in July 1986 is Boeing 727-22 N7065U (c/n 18872). This aircraft is currently operated as a freighter by one of the large US parcel carriers.

Florida-based Amerijet International is an all-cargo carrier. Pictured at Miami, in June 1989, is Boeing 727-51F N5607 (c/n 18804). This airframe is currently in service with a Colombian freight airline.

American Airlines is the largest airline in the world. Pictured at Dayton, Ohio in July 1986 is Boeing 727-23 N1972 (c/n 18428). This aircraft was sold on and eventually reduced to spares in 1999.

Dallas, Texas-based Express One International was a cargo carrier. Pictured at Philadelphia, on a wet day in May 1989, is Boeing 727-31F N220NE (c/n 18905). The company suspended services in 2002. Although retaining its US registration, this aircraft was recently flying in Venezuela.

Based at Marana, Arizona, Evergreen International Airlines have an all-cargo fleet. Pictured at base in September 1988 is Boeing 727-46F N745EV (c/n 19283). This aircraft was withdrawn at this long-term storage facility in 1992 and was still to be seen there some fourteen years later.

When one airline leases an aircraft from another for short periods it will usually only carry a hybrid scheme as the cost of a full repaint is too high for the time frame. One example of this is Boeing 727-22 N284AT (c/n 19151) of American Trans Air on lease to British Airways, which is in ATA colours with BA titles. It is of note that the 727 is the one Boeing type that BA has not had in its fleet. N284AT is pictured at London-Gatwick in July 1988, near the end of a three-month lease. This aircraft was sold on and, after service in Peru, was used for ground instruction by a technical school at Tucson, Arizona.

UPS Airlines is a division of the United Parcel Service Company of Louisville, Kentucky. They currently operate a large fleet of several hundred aircraft from a 727 to a 747. Pictured landing at Los Angeles-LAX in October 1984 is Boeing 727-22C N928UP (c/n 19091). This aircraft still serves the company having been re-engined with R-R Tays to reduce both noise and fuel burn.

Pictured at Melbourne, Australia in February 1981 is Boeing 727-77C C2-RN4 (c/n 20370) of Air Nauru, the sole airline of the Pacific island state. The carrier currently does not have any aircraft in its fleet but leases them from regional operators for its services. This airframe is currently a freighter in Angola. (Bob O'Brien)

Canadian carrier **First Air** operates a mixed fleet of combi aircraft, enabling it to carry both passengers and freight on the same flight, mostly to the sparsely inhabited far north of the country. Pictured on a passenger charter to Phoenix, Arizona in September 1988 is Boeing 727-44C C-GVFA (c/n 20475). This aircraft is currently operated by an African carrier.

Despite its name **Alaskan Airlines** is based in Seattle, Washington. Pictured there in September 1984 is Boeing 727-27 N293AS (c/n 19534). This aircraft was sold on to a carrier in Venezuela and is reported to have been withdrawn from use.

Lisbon-based **TAP – Transportes Aereos Portugueses** is the national flag carrier for the nation and currently has an all-Airbus fleet. Pictured operating a holiday charter to Liverpool-Speke in June 1981 is Boeing 727-155C CS-TBV (c/n 19618). This aircraft was sold on, converted to a freighter, withdrawn and is in store at Kingman, Arizona.

Pictured landing at New York-JFK in May 1989 is Boeing 727-22C N727CK (c/n 19195) of Connie Kalitta Services. The freight carrier was based at Detroit-Willow Run and specialised in shipping for the local motor industry. The company, headed by Conrad Kalitta, a well-known drag race driver, changed its name to American International and later merged with Kitty Hawk. When the latter company hit financial trouble, Conrad returned to the aviation scene and acquired its operating rights for new company Kalitta Air. This aircraft is currently in service with an Alaskan-based company.

First flown in July 1967, the -200 series of the 727 had two 10ft (3.05m) fuselage sections added, one ahead and one aft of the wing. It was the best-selling version, with 1258 airframes constructed. In a high-density seating configuration 189 passengers could be accommodated. Pictured at Boston in August 1986 is Boeing 727-243 N576PE (c/n 21269) of PEOPLExpress. This pioneer of low-cost, no-frills travel grew so fast that its Newark, New Jersey, base could not handle the passenger numbers. In February 1987 they were taken over by Continental Airlines. This aircraft is currently in service as a freighter with an American company.

Perhaps the best known of all US carriers was Pan American World Airways. Pictured at Zurich in August 1987 is Boeing 727-235 N4743 (c/n 19463). The airline, famous for its early 707 and 747 operations, ceased trading in December 1991. This aircraft was withdrawn from use at the end of the company's life and broken up for spare parts two years later.

Pictured landing at Miami in October 1981 is Boeing 727-231 N54353 (c/n 21985) of TWA – Trans World Airways. The old-established carrier was taken over by American Airlines in 2001 and this aircraft is in store at Tucson, Arizona.

Operating a leased Peruvian-registered Boeing 727-247 OB-1301 (c/n 20263) at Miami in June 1989 is **Haiti Trans Air**. They operated passenger flights from Port-au-Prince and suspended services in October 1995. This aircraft was withdrawn from use in Lima.

Like many South American airlines **Avensa (Aerovias Venezolanas SA)** have a long history, being formed in 1943. They currently operate just a single aircraft. Pictured at Miami, in June 1989, is Boeing 727-2D3 YV-97C (c/n 20885). This aircraft is believed to have been withdrawn from use.

LAB – Lloyd Aereo Boliviano was formed in 1925, making it one of the oldest airlines in South America. Pictured at Miami in June 1989 is Boeing 727-2K3 CP-1276 (c/n 21082). This aircraft still serves the company.

The main passenger carrier of Honduras TAN (Transportes Aereos Nacionales) operated around Central America and to Miami in the USA where Boeing 727-224 N88705 (c/n 19514) is pictured in June 1989. In 1991 the airline merged with another Tegucigalpa-based carrier and took their name, SAHSA. This aircraft crashed in Honduras in October 1989.

Texas-based Braniff was an innovator when it came to airline liveries. The same basic scheme was used, but in several different colours. Seen at Miami in October 1981 is Boeing 727-227 N465BN (c/n 21492). The following year operations were suspended. This aircraft was converted to a freighter and is now operated by a major US parcel carrier.

Just to show you cannot keep a good airline down, Braniff returned in 1984 with a new livery. Pictured at Phoenix, Arizona in September 1988 is Boeing 727-227 N462BN (c/n 21489). Sadly the carrier finally closed down in November 1989. This aircraft, like the one pictured above, was converted to a freighter and serves as a parcel carrier in the USA.

Houston, Texas-based Continental Airlines is one of America's oldest carriers, being formed in 1934, and today is also one of its largest. Pictured at Washington-National in May 1989 is Boeing 727-243 N580PE (c/n 21663). It was sold on, converted to a freighter and now serves with a Canadian carrier.

Southwest Airlines are famous for their pioneering high-frequency, low-cost, no-frills flying together with a sense of fun. They are also known for the use of a single type of aircraft, the Boeing 737. For a short period they did however operate a small number of 727s. Pictured at Los Angeles-LAX in October 1984 is Boeing 727-227 N551PE (c/n 20772). This aircraft is currently working as a freighter in Canada.

Pictured at Nairobi in August 1980 is Boeing 727-2F9 5N-ANQ (c/n 21427) of Nigerian Airways. Once the flag carrier for the country they suspended operations in 2003. This aircraft currently operates as a freighter in Colombia. (Bob O'Brien)

Wien Air Alaska flew scheduled passenger services around its state and to the 'lower 48'. Pictured at Seattle-Tacoma in September 1984 is Boeing 727-277 N275WC (c/n 20549). Operations were suspended later that year and this aircraft is currently a freighter in Australia.

Flying a holiday charter to the UK is Portuguese carrier Air Atlantis; they were based at Faro in the Algarve region. Pictured at London-Gatwick in July 1987 is Boeing 727-232 CS-TCH (c/n 20866). The airline suspended operations in April 1993, this aircraft was converted to a freighter and crashed in Florida in July 2002.

Dutch charter carrier Air Holland was based at Amsterdam-Schiphol and at the time when operations were suspended in 1999 operated an all-Boeing fleet. Pictured at Zurich in August 1987 is Boeing 727-2H3 PH-AHB (c/n 20739). This aircraft was sold on to an airline in Colombia and is currently preserved at the Parque Sautre Magico in Bogotá.

Minneapolis-St Paul-based Republic Airlines was formed in 1979 following the merger of several carriers. Pictured at Boston in August 1986 is Boeing 727-2M7 N725RW (c/n 21502). This was the year that they were taken over by their neighbours, Northwest Airlines. This aircraft was sold on, converted to a freighter, withdrawn and stored at Roswell, New Mexico.

The best-selling jet airliner to date is the Boeing 737. It first flew in April 1967 and there have been nine different variants in passenger service. Only thirty of the original - 100 series were sold, but the -200 became the standard production machine with over 1000 manufactured. Pictured at its Bangkok base in November 1989 is Boeing 737-2P5 HS-TBE (c/n 23113) of Thai Airways. This aircraft was sold on, operated in Panama, and is currently to be found flying passengers in Indonesia.

Still the best of the low-cost carriers, Southwest Airlines is also the most copied. Pictured at Phoenix, Arizona in September 1988 is Boeing 737-2H4 N103SW (c/n 23109). This aircraft is currently flying passengers for a Beirut-based airline.

Midway Airlines was one of the carriers that grew up following deregulation by operating from the then under-used downtown airports: in their case Chicago-Midway, hence the name. Pictured at Miami in June 1989 is Boeing 737-2T4 N703ML (c/n 22529). The company suspended its services in November 1991; although in 1993 its name was acquired by another airline. This aircraft was sold on and currently carries passengers for an Arizona-based airline.

Pictured at Melbourne-Tullamarine in March 1985 is Boeing 737-2L7C C2-RN3 (c/n 21073) of **Air Nauru**. It is of note that the Pacific island-based carrier has a mix of alphabetical and numeric characters in its registration. This aircraft was sold on to a Brazilian company and is believed to have been withdrawn from service. (Bob O'Brien)

Tunisair is the flag carrier for the Republic of Tunisia and is based in the capital city Tunis. Currently the airline operates both Boeing and Airbus aircraft. Pictured at Manchester-Ringway in September 1984 is Boeing 737-2H3 TS-IOE (c/n 22624). This aircraft is still owned by the company but is in store at their base.

Delhi-based **Indian Airlines** mostly fly domestic services but some regional international passenger operations are flown. On one such flight at Bangkok in November 1989 is Boeing 737-2A8 VT-EFL (c/n 21497). This aircraft crashed in India in August 1991.

Egyptian carrier **Air Sinai** today leases aircraft from Egyptair as required. Pictured on the ramp at its Cairo base in June 1988 is Boeing 737-266 SU-AYO (c/n 21227). This aircraft currently operates for an Indonesian airline.

Pictured at Miami in October 1981 is Boeing 737-2A1 YS-08C (c/n 21599) of the El Salvador carrier **TACA**. The airline now operates in several Central and South American countries. This aircraft currently operates for a Lagos, Nigeria-based airline.

The Irish flag carrier **Aer Lingus** dates back to 1936 and today has an all-Airbus fleet. Pictured at Manchester-Ringway in April 1989 is Boeing 737-248C EI-ASL (c/n 21011). This aircraft currently operates for a Canadian airline in a combi passenger/freight role.

Quebecair was based in the Canadian province and operated scheduled passenger services both around the country and to the USA. Pictured at Toronto in July 1986 is Boeing 737-296 C-GQBB (c/n 22276). The carrier later became part of Canadian Airlines International while this aircraft is currently flying passengers for an airline in Chile.

Nova Scotia-based **EPA (Eastern Provincial Airways)** was one of the carriers that formed Canadian Airlines International in 1987. Pictured prior to this, at Toronto in July 1986, is Boeing 737-2E1 C-FEPO (c/n 20300). Sold on, this aircraft is currently in store in California.

British holiday charter operator **Britannia Airways** was the launch operator of the 737 in the UK. Their first aircraft was delivered in July 1968. Pictured at Manchester-Ringway in October 1982 is Boeing 737-204 G-AVRN (c/n 19711). The carrier now operates under the name Thomsonfly. This aircraft was sold on and, following its most recent use in the Philippines, is currently in store at Taipei.

An associate company of TEA Belgium, TEA UK (Trans European Airways) flew passenger charters around Europe. Pictured at Manchester-Ringway in March 1989 is Boeing 737-2M8 G-BTEB (c/n 21736). The company, based at Birmingham, ceased operations in September 1991. This aircraft currently has an Icelandic registration and is in store at Casablanca, Morocco.

Vancouver, British Columbia-based Pacific Western Airlines flew across Canada and into the USA, operating scheduled passenger services. Pictured at Toronto in July 1986 is Boeing 737-275 C-GUPW (c/n 22873). April of the following year saw the carrier become one of the founders of Canadian Airlines International. This aircraft is currently in store in California.

Quebec-based **Nordair** was another of the smaller carriers that were to merge to form Canadian Airlines International in April 1987. Pictured at Toronto in July 1986 is Boeing 737-242 C-GNDR (c/n 22075). Sold on, this airframe crashed in Afghanistan in February 2005.

Cardiff-based carrier **Airways International Cymru** had a short life span, from 1984 to 1988. (Cymru is Wales in the Welsh language.) Pictured on a holiday charter flight at London-Gatwick in July 1987 is Boeing 737-204 G-BAZI (c/n 20808). This aircraft is currently operated by a Chilean airline.

GB Airways Boeing 737-2S3 G-DDDV (c/n 22633) is pictured at London-Gatwick in July 1988. The company now flies an all-Airbus fleet as a British Airways franchise carrier with its aircraft in BA livery. This aircraft was sold on to an airline in the Argentine and was in store at Buenos Aires at the end of 2003.

Miami-based **Air Florida** flew both short-haul domestic and long-haul international services. Pictured at Tampa, Florida in October 1981 is Boeing 737-222 N63AF (c/n 19553). The airline merged with Midway and this aircraft was operated in various parts of the world before being withdrawn and broken up for spare parts in 2000.

Greek national flag carrier **Olympic Airways** Boeing 737-284 SX-BCI (c/n 22343) is pictured at Düsseldorf, Germany in June 1983. The company now use the name 'Airlines' rather than 'Airways'. This aircraft was withdrawn and, following a period of storage, is currently operated by an Indonesian airline.

One of the most famous names in Canadian transport is that of Canadian Pacific. It was involved in rail transport as well as air, and even had a song written about it. Pictured at Toronto in July 1986 is Boeing 737-217 C-GCPO (c/n 21718) in the old livery of the airline. The following year the carrier was one of the group that formed Canadian Airlines International. This aircraft is currently in store in California.

To maintain the success of the 737 Boeing introduced the -300 series. First flown in February 1984, it had a fuselage extension of 104in (2.6m) and new engines. These were CFM-56 turbofans of 22,100lb static thrust. A total of 1025 -300s were built. Pictured at Toronto in July 1986 is Boeing 737-317 C-FCPL (c/n 23177) in the new colours of Canadian Pacific Air Lines. Note that, on this side of the aircraft, the titles have a French language spelling. This aircraft currently serves with a Russian airline.

Once one of the oldest airlines in America, Western Airlines had a history dating back to 1925. Pictured at Billings, Montana, in August 1986, is Boeing 737-347 N3301 (c/n 23181). In April of the following year the carrier was taken over by Delta Air Lines who operated this aircraft until it went to a Mexican low-cost carrier in 2006.

Set up by Horizon Travel to fly its holidaymakers around the sun spots of Europe, Orion Airways was based at East Midlands-Castle Donington. Pictured landing at Manchester-Ringway in April 1989 is Boeing 737-3T0 G-BOLM (c/n 23942). It was during this year that the company was bought out by Thomson Holidays and merged into their own house airline Britannia Airways. This aircraft currently serves with a major US passenger carrier.

First at Stavanger and then at Oslo, Norway Airlines had a fleet of two aircraft for charter operations. Pictured at London-Gatwick in July 1988 is Boeing 737-33A LN-NOS (c/n 23830). The company operated the following year as Air Europe Scandinavia before reverting to its original name. October 1992 saw the end of operations and this aircraft currently operates for a Brazilian passenger carrier.

Pictured landing at Manchester-Ringway in April 1989 is Boeing 737-33A LN-NOR (c/n 23827) of Air Europe Scandinavia. This Stavanger-based carrier was a member of the Airlines of Europe Group and an associate of the UK Leisure Group. March 1991 saw the name change back to Norway Airlines. This aircraft has now been fitted with blended winglets and serves with a German airline.

Formed in 1947, JAT (Jugoslovenski Aero Transport) was the national flag carrier for Yugoslavia. Pictured at Luton in September 1988 is Boeing 737-3H9 YU-AND (c/n 23329). The Belgrade-based carrier now only represents the state of Serbia following the civil war that tore the old country into separate republics. This aircraft still serves the airline, now known as JAT Airways.

Le Bourget-based French carrier **Aéromaritime International** operated an all-Boeing fleet. Pictured at Manchester-Ringway in July 1989 is Boeing 737-33A F-GFUD (c/n 24027). The airline was merged into Air France at the end of 1992 and this aircraft is currently owned by a Spanish carrier.

Boeing first flew the 737-400 in February 1988. It was a further stretch on the -300 series of 114in (2.89m), the CFM-56 now had a power output of 23,500lb static thrust and the aircraft a higher gross take-off weight. Seating capacity rose to 168 and a total of 440 were constructed. Pictured at East Midlands-Castle Donington in June 1989 is Boeing 737-4Y0 G-UKLB (c/n 24344) of **Air UK Leisure**. This was the charter arm of scheduled carrier Air UK. In February 1997 it merged into Leisure International Airways and this aircraft is currently with a Dutch passenger airline.

First flown in July 1975, six years after the original -100 series, the Boeing 747SP (Special Performance) was 48ft (14.63m) shorter but had a very long range. It did not sell well, with just forty-eight constructed. Pictured at London-Gatwick in July 1987 is Boeing 747-SP27 N1301E (c/n 22302) of CAAC (Civil Aviation Administration of China). At one time it was the sole airline of the country, in much the same way as Aeroflot in the USSR, but by the end of the 1980s regional self-managed airlines had started operations. This aircraft was sold on, withdrawn and stored in Indonesia in 2002.

First flown in February 1969, the Boeing 747, universally known as the 'Jumbo-Jet', is the best known and best selling of all the wide-body jets. The aircraft is still in production with the -400 series. Pictured landing at New York-JFK in May 1989 is Boeing 747-131 N93108 (c/n 19674) of TWA – Trans World Airlines. This aircraft stayed with the carrier all its life: withdrawn and stored at Marana, Arizona in 1998, it was broken up there two years later.

The Belgian flag carrier Sabena (Societe Anonyme Belge d'Exploitation de la Navigation Aerienne) operated from 1923 until November 2001 when services were suspended. Pictured at London-Gatwick in July 1987 is Boeing 747-129A OO-SGB (c/n 20402). This aircraft was sold on, withdrawn, stored at Mojave, California in 1994 and broken up four years later.

Pictured on approach to land at New York-JFK in May 1989 is Boeing 747-128 F-BPVA (c/n 19749) of Air France. The carrier was formed in 1933 and is the largest airline in Europe following its acquisition of KLM. This aircraft was sold on and broken up for spare parts in Oklahoma during 1994.

The -200 series of the 747 had an increased gross take-off weight, extra fuel capacity and a stronger airframe. The airlines buying it could select from three different power plants. The charter arm of British Airways, British Airtours had started life as BEA Airtours in 1969 and following the BEA/BOAC merger took the present name. Pictured at Manchester-Ringway in September 1984 is Boeing 747-236B G-BDXL (c/n 22305). This aircraft, in an all-economy-seat configuration, was operating a flight to Los Angeles. The carrier changed its name, in April 1988, to Caledonian following the BA take-over of British Caledonian. This aircraft was later operated by an Icelandic company and is currently in store in Arizona.

ANA – All Nippon Airways is one of the two major carriers in Japan. Pictured at Los Angeles-LAX in September 1988 is Boeing 747-281B JA8182 (c/n 23813). This aircraft was converted to a freighter and currently serves with NCA – Nippon Cargo Airlines, an associate company of ANA.

It is not a common sight to see a 747 performing at an airshow but Northwest Orient Airlines Boeing 747-251B N636US (c/n 23547) is pictured displaying at Oshkosh, Wisconsin in August 1986. Minneapolis-St Paul's main based carrier, now just known as Northwest Airlines, still owns this aircraft albeit in store in Arizona.

Once Britain's second carrier with domestic and both long- and short-haul international services British Caledonian Air Lines was taken over by BA in April 1988. Pictured at their London-Gatwick base in the previous July is Boeing 747-211B G-NIGB (c/n 21517). This aircraft was last used in the Philippines and was broken up in Arizona during April 2006.

Pictured on approach to New York-JFK in May 1989 is Boeing 747-287B LV-OEP (c/n 22297) of Buenos Aires-based Aerolineas Argentinas. This aircraft is still operated by the airline.

Spanish carrier Iberia (Lineas Aereas de Espana) dates back to 1927, the bulk of their current fleet being Airbus designs. Pictured at New York-JFK in May 1989 is Boeing 747-256B EC-DLD (c/n 22455). This aircraft is still owned by the airline and is currently in store at their Madrid base.

PEOPLExpress Boeing 747-243B N605PE (c/n 20520) is pictured at London-Gatwick in July 1986. The low-cost, long- and short-haul carrier was taken over by Continental Airlines in February of the following year. This aircraft is in store in Arizona in the process of being broken up for spare parts.

Still in service today with the same carrier, albeit as a freighter, is Japan Air Lines Boeing 747-246B JA8169 (c/n 23389). It is pictured landing at New York-JFK in May 1989, when still in passenger configuration.

Seoul-based Korean Air Boeing 747-2B5B HL7458 (c/n 22485) is pictured at Zurich in August 1987. This aircraft was converted to a freight role and currently serves in Israel.

Pan American World Airways was the first operator of the 747 in passenger service. Pictured at Miami in October 1981 is Boeing 747-221F N905PA (c/n 21744) operated by Pan Am Cargo. The -200F version had a nose cargo door that opened upwards as well as a door on the rear port side, there were no cabin windows. This aircraft is currently serving as a freighter in Japan.

Garuda Indonesia is the Jakarta-based flag carrier for the nation. Pictured arriving at Zurich in August 1987 is Boeing 747-2U3B PK-GSE (c/n 22768). This aircraft was sold on, converted to a freighter and written off in a landing accident at Medellin, Colombia in June 2006 whilst being operated by an American carrier.

Pictured landing at Miami in June 1989 is Virgin Atlantic Airways Boeing 747-287B G-VIRG (c/n 21189). This carrier has always had a high publicity profile thanks to its founder Richard (now Sir Richard) Branson. This aircraft was sold on and is now in service with a Nigerian carrier.

The -300 series 747 had a stretched upper deck together with a higher gross take-off weight. Once again there was a choice of three engine manufacturers. Pictured at its Zurich base in August 1987 is Boeing 747-357 N221GF (c/n 22996) of Swissair. It came as a surprise to many when this well-known and respected carrier ceased operations in March 2002. This aircraft currently serves with an Icelandic airline.

Boeing's 757 is a medium-range, narrow-body airliner that first flew in February 1982. Power came from either a pair of Rolls-Royce RB.211s or Pratt & Whitney PW2037 engines. Service entry was with Eastern Air Lines in January 1983 and with British Airways the following month. Pictured at Washington-National in May 1989 is Boeing 757-232 N627DL (c/n 22917) of Delta Air Lines. This aircraft still serves with the Atlanta-based carrier.

Phoenix, Arizona-based America West Airlines was formed in 1981 and has grown to a size where it took over its larger competitor, US Airways. Pictured at base in September 1988 is Boeing 757-2S7 N905AW (c/n 23567). This aircraft is still current with the company and has recently been repainted as US Airways, as the new joint company is to be known.

The 757 has proven to be a popular aircraft with the holiday charter carriers as it can be configured to hold up to 235 passengers in all-economy seating. Pictured on approach to Manchester-Ringway in April 1989 is Boeing 757-2T7 G-MONB (c/n 22780) of Luton-based, British holiday charter company Monarch Airlines. This aircraft still serves the airline.

Once a major player in the UK holiday charter market, Air Europe ceased operations in March 1991. Pictured on pushback at Manchester-Ringway in April 1987 is Boeing 757-236 G-BLVH (c/n 23227). This aircraft was sold on, operated in the USA and is currently in store to be broken up for spare parts.

CAAC (Civil Aviation Administration of China) used to operate all civil flying in the country; the end of the 1980s saw regional carriers emerge. Pictured at Bangkok in November 1989 is Boeing 757-21B B-2804 (c/n 24330) in full CAAC livery. This aircraft now operates for Guangzhou-based China Southern Airlines.

A twin-engine, wide-body airliner the Boeing 767 first flew in September 1981. All three major engine manufactures, Rolls-Royce, General Electric and Pratt & Whitney, offered power plant options. Pictured landing at Los Angeles-LAX in September 1988 is Boeing 767-222 N618UA (c/n 21878) of United Airlines. This aircraft is still owned by the company but is in store at Victorville, California.

It is of note that both the People's Republic of China and the Republic of China (Taiwan) have the same registration prefix for their fleets of airliners despite the different outlooks, claims and governments of the 'two' Chinas. Formed in 1959, **China Airlines** is the largest carrier in Taiwan. Pictured at Bangkok in November 1989 is Boeing 767-209 B-1836 (c/n 22681). The airline has since introduced a new livery, while this aircraft now serves a Canadian carrier.

TACA of El Salvador first operated the 767 in 1986. Pictured at Miami in June 1989 is Boeing 767-251 N767TA (c/n 23494). The carrier now operates an all-Airbus fleet and this aircraft was damaged beyond economic repair after overrunning the runway at Guatemala City in April 1993.

Additional fuel tanks gave the 767 a new 'Extended Range' version that has sold well with the airlines. Pictured landing at Manchester-Ringway in April 1989 is Boeing 767-204(ER) G-BNYS (c/n 24013) of UK holiday charter carrier **Britannia Airways**. The company fitted 290 seat into this variant. They now operate under the name of Thomsonfly and this aircraft has been sold on to another British charter airline.

Once just a US domestic carrier, Piedmont Airlines ordered the 767 in 1986 to start services to the UK during the following year. Boeing 767-201(ER) N604P (c/n 23898) is pictured at London-Gatwick in July 1987. Two years later the company was renamed US Air; this aircraft still serves the airline.

American Airlines first operated the 767 at the end of 1982 and currently operate sixteen -200 series and fifty-eight of the stretched -300 series, all are Extended Range versions. Pictured at Manchester-Ringway in April 1987 is Boeing 767-233(ER) N321AA (c/n 22322). This aircraft is still current in the fleet.

Israel's flag carrier El Al first operated the 767 in 1983. Pictured at Zurich in August 1987 is Boeing 767-258(ER) 4X-EAD (c/n 22975). It still serves with the airline.

The Douglas DC-9 followed on from the Caravelle and BAC One-Eleven as a jet-powered, short-haul airliner. Due to the company's ability to stretch the fuselage, as demand for more and more seats grew, it outsold both of its rivals by a large margin. It first flew in February 1965 and the original -10 series was 104ft (31.7m) long. Pictured at East Midlands-Castle Donington in June 1987 is Douglas DC-9-15 G-BMAA (c/n 47048) of British Midland. This carrier operated both domestic and European services with the type, and they now brand themselves bmi. This aircraft was sold on to a Colombian airline and is currently in store at Bogotá.

Founded in St Louis, Missouri in 1946 Ozark Air Lines grew to be a large domestic carrier. Pictured landing at Miami in October 1981 is DC-9-15 N907Z (c/n 45772). The company was taken over by TWA in 1986 and this aircraft was withdrawn from use in 1999 and broken up for spare parts three years later.

Pictured at its home base of Reno-Cannon, Nevada in September 1988 is DC-9-15 N1068T (c/n 45782) of Great American Airways. The carrier was formed in 1979, conducted domestic passenger services, grew to a fleet of nine and suspended operations in April 1997. This aircraft was sold to a Mexican airline and withdrawn from service in 2002.

The -30 series of the DC-9 was stretched by 15ft (4.7m) to give a seating capacity of 115 passengers. Pictured landing at Miami in October 1981 is DC-9-31 N963N (c/n 47415) of Republic Airlines. Based in Minneapolis-St Paul, the company had been formed by the 1979 merger of North Central Airlines and Southern Airways. Republic were themselves taken over in 1986 by the other Minneapolis-based carrier Northwest Airlines. This aircraft still serves with the new owner.

Pictured at Washington-National in May 1989 is DC-9-31 N920VJ (c/n 48140) of US Air. The carrier now calls itself US Airways while this aircraft is currently operated by a Nigerian airline based in Lagos.

Named after its home base of Chicago's Midway Airport, Midway Airlines was one of the carriers that grew by using the small, older, under-used inner city airports rather than the new larger ones miles out from the centres. Pictured at Washington-National in May 1989 is Douglas DC-9-31 N937ML (c/n 47005). The company ceased operations in November 1991. Two years later a completely new airline, at the same location, re-used the name and commenced services. This aircraft is currently flown by an company in the Venezuelan capital of Caracas.

A charter flying subsidiary of Alitalia, Naples-based **ATI – Aero Transporti Italiani** was founded in 1963 and merged into its parent in November 1994. Seen here at London-Gatwick in July 1987 is DC-9-32 I-ATIQ (c/n 47591). This aircraft was sold on and is currently in store in Arizona.

Wilmington, Ohio-based **Airborne Express** is one of the larger US freight and parcel carriers. They were formed in 1980 and currently operate with the new name ABX Air. Pictured at Miami in August 1986 is Douglas DC-9-32CF N905AX (c/n 47147). This variant is convertible to both cargo and passenger use as it retains cabin windows; it still serves with the company.

La Guardia-based **New York Air** was one of the operators that grew following the American airline industry deregulation. They flew high-frequency, low-fare passenger operations. Pictured at Boston in August 1986 is DC-9-32 N535TX (c/n 47111). The carrier was owned by the Texas Air Corporation who merged them into Continental Airlines the following year. This aircraft was withdrawn and stored in 2000 and broken up at Mojave, California in 2001.

A holiday charter subsidiary of Spanish flag carrier Iberia, Aviaco (Aviacion y Comercio SA) was formed in 1948. Pictured at Düsseldorf in June 1983 is Douglas DC-9-32 EC-CGN (c/n 47637). The airline was merged into its parent in September 1999 and this aircraft was withdrawn from use at Madrid in 2001 and broken up the following year.

Inex Adria Aviopromet used to be one of the leading holiday charter airlines of Yugoslavia. Following the violent disintegration of the republic they have evolved into Adria Airways of Slovenia. Pictured at Manchester-Ringway in October 1982 is Douglas DC-9-33 YU-AHW (c/n 47530). This aircraft is currently in store at Naples.

Dating back to 1919 the Dutch flag carrier KLM (Koninklijke Luchtvaart Maatschappij) is one of the best known airlines of the world. Pictured at London-Gatwick in July 1987 is DC-9-33 PH-DNP (c/n 47194). KLM has merged with Air France but the two carriers continue to operate in their respective liveries. This aircraft was converted to a freighter and is currently operated by a US cargo airline.

The national airline of Sweden, Norway and Denmark, SAS – Scandinavian Airlines System is one of the few multi-nation airlines of the world. Pictured at Manchester-Ringway in October 1982 is DC-9-41 LN-RLU (c/n 47511). The -40 series was stretched to 125ft 7in (38.25m) and could seat up to 125 passengers. This aircraft was converted to a freighter and is currently operated by a large US parcel company.

Last of the true DC-9 versions was the -50 series. This was once again stretched, this time by 96in (2.44m), bringing it to a total length of 133ft 7in (40.7m). The type had grown by 29ft 2in (8.84m) from the original -10 series. Pictured at Zurich in August 1987 is DC-9-51 OH-LYN (c/n 47694) of the Finnish flag carrier Finnair. This aircraft is currently operated in a 135-passenger layout by a Venezuelan airline.

In April 1967 the Douglas company merged with McDonnell to become McDonnell Douglas. The final stretch of the DC-9 first flew in October 1979 and took the new marketing name of MD-80. The stretch was 14ft 3in (4.34m) bringing it to 147ft 10in (45.06m), with a capacity of 172 seats. The MD-82 was the same length but with uprated engines, having Pratt & Whitney JT8D-217 turbofans with 20,000lb static thrust. Pictured at London-Heathrow in May 1988 is McDonnell Douglas MD-82 I-DAWH (c/n 49202) of the Italian flag carrier Alitalia. This aircraft is still in service with the airline.

The name Frontier has been a popular title for an airline. Pictured at Seattle-Tacoma in August 1986 is McDonnell Douglas MD-82 N9804F (c/n 49114) of Denver, Colorado-based Frontier Airlines. It was in this month that the carrier was taken over by Continental Airlines. This aircraft is currently in service with an Indonesian company.

Pictured landing at Los Angeles-LAX in September 1988 is McDonnell Douglas MD-82 N821US (c/n 49138) in a hybrid livery of PSA – Pacific Southwest Airlines colours with US Air titles, PSA having been taken over by US Air earlier in the year. Sold on, this aircraft is currently in service with a Turkish airline.

The 1979 deregulation of America's airlines was the catalyst for growth for many carriers. One such was Orange County-based Air Cal. Pictured at Seattle-Tacoma in September 1984 is McDonnell Douglas MD-82 N479AC (c/n 48066). The airline was taken over by American Airlines in 1987 and this aircraft currently serves a Dubrovnik-based Croatian airline.

Following their takeover of Muse Air, Southwest Airlines renamed it **TranStar Airlines**. The Dallas-Love Field-based carrier flew high-frequency passenger services in the southwest region of the USA. Pictured at Los Angeles-LAX in August 1986 is McDonnell Douglas MD-82 N930MC (c/n 48056). In August 1989 services were suspended and this aircraft is currently in store.

Curacao-based, in the Netherland Antilles, **ALM – Antillean Airlines** (Antilliaanse Luchtvaart Maatschappij) flew regional passenger services. Pictured at Miami in June 1989 is McDonnell Douglas MD-82 PJ-SEG (c/n 49124). The carrier was renamed DCA-Dutch Caribbean Airlines and eventually ceased operations in October 2004. This aircraft is currently in store in Mexico City.

To increase the range of the type the manufacturer added two belly fuel tanks; this variant was the MD-83. Pictured at London-Gatwick in July 1988 is McDonnell Douglas MD-83 G-BNSA (c/n 49643) of **BIA – British Island Airways**. The carrier operated scheduled passenger services in the UK including the Channel Islands and the Isle of Man. Operations were suspended in 1990 and this aircraft currently operates for a Las Vegas-based airline.

The Douglas DC-8 was first flown in May 1958 and due to its excellent design has outlasted its rivals, the Boeing 707 and Convair 880. The fuselage was capable of being stretched and following engine replacements, with modern CFM-56s, many DC-8s serve to this day with major cargo carriers. Pictured at Miami in October 1981 is Douglas DC-8-32 HC-BEI (c/n 45606) of Andes Airlines. This company was based in the city of Guayaquil in Ecuador and was an all-freight carrier. Operations were suspended in 1998, while this aircraft had been withdrawn and broken up at base in 1985.

Based in Benin City, Nigeria was Flash Airlines, an all-cargo carrier that had been set up in 1985. Pictured at London-Gatwick in July 1988 is Douglas DC-8-55F 5N-ATZ (c/n 45965). The company suspended its operations in October 1996 and this aircraft was damaged beyond economic repair at Port Harcourt, Nigeria in December 1996.

One of the best known DC-8 cargo carriers was Miami-based Airlift International. Pictured at base in October 1981 is DC-8-54F N108RD (c/n 45663). The company suspended operations in 1992 and this aircraft is currently in store in Luanda, Angola.

ARCA – Aerovias Colombianas was a Colombian freight carrier, based in Bogotá. Pictured at Miami in June 1989 is DC-8-51F HK-2587X (c/n 45635). The company suspended operations in January 1997, this aircraft had been withdrawn from use at Miami in 1988 and later scrapped.

Pictured at Miami in October 1981 is Douglas DC-8-55F OB-R-1200 (c/n 45882) of Lima-based Aeronaves del Peru. The company had a life span of almost thirty years, from being formed in 1965 to the suspension of operations in August 1994. This aircraft was sold on and crashed in Paraguay in February 1996.

Founded in 1974, **LAC – Lineas Aereas del Caribe** was a cargo carrier based at Barranquilla on Colombia's Caribbean coast. Pictured at Miami in October 1981 is DC-8-54F HK-2380 (c/n 45879). The company ceased operations in 1996 and this aircraft was damaged beyond economic repair after it overran the runway, at base, in September 1984.

Spantax were for many years one of the best known Spanish holiday charter operators, first with piston-powered DC-6s and DC-7s and later with jets. Pictured at Zurich in August 1987 is Douglas DC-8-61 EC-DVB (c/n 46037). The -60 series of the DC-8 was stretched by 20ft (6.1m) forward of the wing and 16ft 8in (5.1m) aft. Maximum passenger numbers went up from 176 to 259. Spantax had a lifespan from 1959 to March 1988, when services were suspended. This aircraft was sold on, converted to a freighter, and currently serves with a major US carrier.

Delta Air Lines of Atlanta, Georgia have for many years been one of the largest passenger carriers in the world. Pictured landing at Miami in October 1981 is DC-8-61 N1307L (c/n 46056). This aircraft was sold on, re-engined, and currently serves a major US parcel carrier.

New York-based **Sea & Sun Airlines** leased DC-8-62H N3931G (c/n 45986) to Los Angeles-based **Pacific East Air**. It is pictured in October 1984 at Marana, Arizona with titles of both airlines. In 1985 Sea & Sun suspended operations; the aircraft was sold on, converted to a freighter and is still operated to the UK by an African carrier.

Surinam Airways is based in the capital Paramaribo. The country of Surinam is the former Dutch Guiana on the mainland of South America. The company was formed in 1954 and today operates an MD-82 for regional and a 747 for long-haul services. Seen at Miami in June 1989 is DC-8-62 N1809E (c/n 46107). Sadly, it crashed on approach to base a few days after this picture was taken.

Braniff was based in Dallas, Texas and had a number of suspensions of operations followed by comebacks over the years. Pictured landing at Miami in October 1981 is DC-8-62 N1804 (c/n 45896). It is in the green scheme, one of a number of solid fuselage colours that the carrier used. In November 1989 the company finally ceased flying and this aircraft was sold on, converted to a freighter, and damaged beyond economic repair when it overran the runway at Singapore in December 2002.

Canadian charter carrier Nationair was based in Montreal. They flew both passenger and cargo services, many of them being to Europe. Pictured at Toronto in July 1986 is DC-8-62 C-GMXY (c/n 45920). In 1993 the company ceased operations, this aircraft was sold on to an African company and is currently in store.

Formed in 1929, **Hawaiian Air** has a long history and today flies an all-Boeing fleet. Pictured, a long way from home, at Zurich in August 1987 is DC-8-62 N8969U (c/n 46070). Sold on, this aircraft was converted to a freighter and is currently in store in New Mexico.

The largest carrier in Canada, following the takeover of Canadian Airlines International, is **Air Canada**. The company operates both domestic and international passenger services. They, at one time, operated dedicated freight aircraft as is illustrated by Douglas DC-8-63AF C-FTIU (c/n 46113). It is pictured at Zurich in August 1987. Sold on, it is currently operated by a US cargo carrier.

One of the earliest 'all-cargo' airlines, **Flying Tigers** was set up in 1945. Pictured landing at Miami in October 1981 is DC-8-63CF N792FT (c/n 46046). The carrier was taken over by Federal Express in August 1989. This aircraft was sold on, re-engined, and is currently serving an American passenger and cargo airline.

Miami-based **Arrow Air** originally flew both passenger and freight charter operations, they then moved on to be an all-cargo carrier. Pictured at base in June 1989 is DC-8-63CF N441J (c/n 45988). The company merged with Fine Air in January 2001 and initially operated under that name, but have since renamed themselves Arrow Cargo. This aircraft still serves the company.

Dutch flag carrier **KLM** had a long history operating the DC-8 in passenger mode. Pictured in June 1983 at the carrier's Amsterdam-Schiphol base is Douglas DC-8-63 PH-DEA (c/n 45903). This aircraft was sold on, converted to a freighter, and is currently in store in Tennessee.

Such was the quality of the DC-8 airframe that many of the -60 series aircraft were re-engined with CFM-56 jets to give extra thrust and reduce both noise and fuel burn. These conversions are known as -70 series. Pictured at Zurich in August 1987 is Douglas DC-8-73CF N801UP (c/n 46101) of **UPS – United Parcel Service**. The Louisville, Kentucky-based parcel carrier is one of the largest such operations in the world. This aircraft still serves with the company.

First flown in August 1970, the McDonnell Douglas DC-10 was a wide-body, twin-aisle airliner powered by three General Electric CF-6 turbofans of 39,300lb static thrust. The launch customer was American Airlines, who ordered twenty-five with the same number of options. They commenced operations with the type in August 1971 with a service from Los Angeles to Chicago. Pictured landing at Los Angeles-LAX in September 1988 is DC-10-10 N154AA (c/n 46709) of American Airlines. This aircraft was sold on, converted to a freighter, and is currently in store awaiting scrapping.

In August 1968 United Airlines ordered sixty DC-10s, half being options. They commenced operations with the type in August 1971. Pictured on approach to Los Angeles-LAX in September 1988 is DC-10-10 N1843U (c/n 46636). This aircraft has been sold on, converted to an MD-10F freighter with an MD-11 'glass' cockpit, and is currently used by a major US parcel carrier.

Pictured at London-Gatwick in July 1987 is DC-10-10 G-GCAL (c/n 46501) of **Cal Air International**. This carrier was set up in October 1985. The company was a holiday charter airline that had evolved from British Caledonian (Charter). The original owners were BCal and the Rank Organisation. When BCal transferred its holidays to Caledonian Leisure the new name was launched. This lasted until December 1988, when the name Novair International Airways was introduced. This aircraft has since been converted to a flying eye hospital for Orbis International. Its role is to transport a team of surgeons to various countries to teach eye surgery and operate on patients. It is based at New York-JFK.

Federal Express first operated the DC-10 in March 1980, today they operate the biggest fleet of the type, with many having been converted to MD-10 standard with two crew and new 'glass' cockpit instrumentation. Pictured landing at Los Angeles-LAX in September 1988 is DC-10-10F N68053 (c/n 47807). This aircraft still serves with the company.

Formed in 1961, Scanair were once the charter arm of Scandinavian Airlines System and flew holiday flights. Based in Stockholm, they operated a fleet of six DC-10s in an all-economy configuration seating 374 passengers. Pictured at Miami in June 1989 is DC-10-10 SE-DHT (c/n 47833). At the start of 1994 the company merged with Conair to form Premiair. This aircraft was withdrawn from use in the UK and broken up for spare parts.

The -30 series of the DC-10 was the long-range variant, the CF-6 turbofans now had a power output of 48,000lb static thrust, and the maximum take-off weight was increased. To cope with the extra load an additional central undercarriage leg was fitted to the fuselage. Pictured at Seattle-Tacoma in August 1986 is DC-10-30 SE-DFD (c/n 46869) of **SAS – Scandinavian Airlines System**. The carrier had first operated the type in November 1974, on the polar route to Japan. This aircraft was sold on, withdrawn from use, and is currently in store at Paris-Orly.

Pictured on take-off from a wet Zurich in August 1987 is DC-10-30(ER) HB-IHN (c/n 48292) of the then Swiss flag carrier **Swissair**. The 'ER' (Extended Range) variant had extra fuel capacity and more powerful engines. This company was the launch customer for this version, receiving the first aircraft in February 1982. Swissair ceased all services in March 2002 and this aircraft was stored and then scrapped in New Mexico.

Holiday charter operator **Balair** was owned by Swissair. Pictured at its Zurich base in August 1987 is DC-10-30 HB-IHK (c/n 46998). The company merged with CTA, was later absorbed into the parent and then re-launched again. This aircraft was sold on, converted to a freighter, and is current with a Miami-based airline.

Pictured landing at its Miami base in October 1981 is DC-10-30 N103SF (c/n 46992) of **Air Florida**. The carrier operated both charter and scheduled passenger flights to both domestic and European destinations. The company merged with Midway in 1984, this aircraft was converted to a freighter and is currently serving with a major US parcel carrier.

Once the dominant carrier at Miami, Eastern Airlines had a history dating back to 1928. The company took over the Miami to London route following the demise of Air Florida. Operations commenced in July 1985 but were discontinued in October of the following year. Pictured at London-Gatwick in July 1986 is DC-10-30 N391EA (c/n 47866). The airline ceased all services in January 1991 and this aircraft was sold on and is in a derelict condition at Mojave, California.

German flag carrier Lufthansa began DC-10 operations in January 1974 on the routes to South America. Pictured at Miami in June 1989 is DC-10-30 D-ADFO (c/n 47925). The airline retired the type in 1994 and this aircraft was sold on, converted to a freighter, and is currently in service with a US carrier.

Condor Flugdienst is a leading German holiday charter operator and was once a subsidiary of Lufthansa. Pictured at Düsseldorf in June 1983 is DC-10-30 D-ADQO (c/n 46596). This aircraft is currently operated by a Tulsa-based airline in an all-economy seating of 380 passengers.

One of the world's leading carriers with regard to cabin service, Thai Airways first operated the DC-10 in April 1975 on routes to Europe. Pictured at Zurich in August 1987 is DC-10-30 HS-TMD (c/n 46961). This aircraft was sold on, and is currently owned by a major US passenger carrier, albeit in store in Arizona.

CP Air, formerly Canadian Pacific was one of the great names in Canadian transport history. Pictured at Toronto in July 1986 is DC-10-30 C-GCPJ (c/n 46991). In April of the following year CP Air was the lead company in the multi-airline merger that produced Canadian Airlines International. This aircraft was sold on, withdrawn in 2001, and scrapped during 2003 at Goodyear, Arizona.

Wardair of Edmonton was a leading charter operator and the first airline to fly the DC-10 in Canada. They started services with the tri-engined wide-body in November 1978. Pictured at London-Gatwick in July 1988 is DC-10-30 C-GXRB (c/n 46976). The company was absorbed into Canadian Airlines International during 1990, this aircraft was sold on, converted to a freighter and is currently serving an airline in Uganda.

Pictured at Miami in June 1989 is DC-10-30 XA-DUG (c/n 46936) of
Aeromexico. The carrier first operated the type in May 1974 on its
route to Madrid from its Mexico City base. This aircraft was sold on,
converted to a freighter and is currently operated by a Lima-based
Peruvian cargo airline.

Once the flag carrier of Venezuela, **VIASA (Venezolana Internacional de
Aviacion)** first operated the DC-10 in April 1974 of services to Europe. Pictured at
Miami in June 1989 is DC-10-30 YV-135C (c/n 46971). In 1997, following mounting
losses, the government-owned airline was closed down. This aircraft was broken
up for spare parts in 1998.

Index of Types

Bibliography

Books

Airbus A300: Gunter Endres; Airlife.

Airlife's Commercial Aircraft & Airliners: Rod Simpson; Airlife.

The Boeing 707, 720 and C-135: Tony Pither; Air Britain.

Jet Airliner Production List Volume 1 & 2 (various editions): Tony Eastwood & John Roach; The Aviation Hobby Shop.

JP Airline Fleets: Ulrich Klee; Bucher & Co, Zurich (various editions).

Lockheed L-1011 TriStar: Philip Birtles; Airlife.

McDonnell Douglas DC-10: Gunter Endres; Airlife.

Piston Engine Airliner Production List (various editions): Tony Eastwood & John Roach; The Aviation Hobby Shop.

Turbo Prop Airliner Production List (various editions): Tony Eastwood & John Roach; The Aviation Hobby Shop.

Magazines

Airliner World, Airliners, Airways, Aviation Letter & Propliner (various editions).